Alternative lending

Alternative Lending

Other Books of Related Interest:

Opposing Viewpoints Series

The Banking Crisis

At Issue Series

Should the Federal Government Bail Out Private Industry?

Current Controversies Series

Consumer Debt

"Congress shall make
no law ... abridging
the freedom of speech,
or of the press."

First Amendment to the U.S. Constitution

The basic foundation of our democracy is the First Amendment guarantee of freedom of expression. The Opposing Viewpoints Series is dedicated to the concept of this basic freedom and the idea that it is more important to practice it than to enshrine it.

OPPOSING
VIEWPOINTS®
SERIES

Alternative Lending

Amanda Hiber, book editor

GREENHAVEN PRESS
A part of Gale, Cengage Learning

GALE
CENGAGE Learning™

Detroit • New York • San Francisco • New Haven, Conn • Waterville, Maine • London

Christine Nasso, *Publisher*
Elizabeth Des Chenes, *Managing Editor*

For more information, contact:
Greenhaven Press
27500 Drake Rd.
Farmington Hills, MI 48331-3535
Or you can visit our Internet site at gale.cengage.com

Articles in Greenhaven Press anthologies are often edited for length to meet page requirements. In addition, original titles of these works are changed to clearly present the main thesis and to explicitly indicate the author's opinion. Every effort is made to ensure that Greenhaven Press accurately reflects the original intent of the authors. Every effort has been made to trace the owners of copyrighted material.

Cover Image copyright © Don Farrall/Digital Vision/Getty Images.

LIBRARY OF CONGRESS CATALOGING-IN-PUBLICATION DATA

Alternative lending / Amanda Hiber, book editor.
    p. cm. -- (Opposing viewpoints)
    Includes bibliographical references and index.
    ISBN 978-0-7377-4753-9 (hardcover) -- ISBN 978-0-7377-4754-6 (pbk.)
    1. Loans--Juvenile literature. I. Hiber, Amanda.
    HG3701.A298 2010
    332.2--dc22
                                            2009046721

Printed in the United States of America
1 2 3 4 5 6 7 14 13 12 11 10

Contents

Chapter 3: Is Peer-to-Peer Lending an Effective Alternative to Traditional Lending?

Chapter 4: Does Microlending Help the Poor?

Why Consider Opposing Viewpoints?

> *"The only way in which a human being can make some approach to knowing the whole of a subject is by hearing what can be said about it by persons of every variety of opinion and studying all modes in which it can be looked at by every character of mind. No wise man ever acquired his wisdom in any mode but this."*
>
> *John Stuart Mill*

In our media-intensive culture it is not difficult to find differing opinions. Thousands of newspapers and magazines and dozens of radio and television talk shows resound with differing points of view. The difficulty lies in deciding which opinion to agree with and which "experts" seem the most credible. The more inundated we become with differing opinions and claims, the more essential it is to hone critical reading and thinking skills to evaluate these ideas. Opposing Viewpoints books address this problem directly by presenting stimulating debates that can be used to enhance and teach these skills. The varied opinions contained in each book examine many different aspects of a single issue. While examining these conveniently edited opposing views, readers can develop critical thinking skills such as the ability to compare and contrast authors' credibility, facts, argumentation styles, use of persuasive techniques, and other stylistic tools. In short, the Opposing Viewpoints Series is an ideal way to attain the higher-level thinking and reading skills so essential in a culture of diverse and contradictory opinions.

In addition to providing a tool for critical thinking, Opposing Viewpoints books challenge readers to question their own strongly held opinions and assumptions. Most people form their opinions on the basis of upbringing, peer pressure, and personal, cultural, or professional bias. By reading carefully balanced opposing views, readers must directly confront new ideas as well as the opinions of those with whom they disagree. This is not to simplistically argue that everyone who reads opposing views will—or should—change his or her opinion. Instead, the series enhances readers' understanding of their own views by encouraging confrontation with opposing ideas. Careful examination of others' views can lead to the readers' understanding of the logical inconsistencies in their own opinions, perspective on why they hold an opinion, and the consideration of the possibility that their opinion requires further evaluation.

Evaluating Other Opinions

To ensure that this type of examination occurs, Opposing Viewpoints books present all types of opinions. Prominent spokespeople on different sides of each issue as well as well-known professionals from many disciplines challenge the reader. An additional goal of the series is to provide a forum for other, less known, or even unpopular viewpoints. The opinion of an ordinary person who has had to make the decision to cut off life support from a terminally ill relative, for example, may be just as valuable and provide just as much insight as a medical ethicist's professional opinion. The editors have two additional purposes in including these less known views. One, the editors encourage readers to respect others' opinions—even when not enhanced by professional credibility. It is only by reading or listening to and objectively evaluating others' ideas that one can determine whether they are worthy of consideration. Two, the inclusion of such viewpoints encourages the important critical thinking skill of objectively evaluating an author's credentials and bias. This evaluation will illuminate an author's reasons for taking a particular stance on an issue and will aid in readers' evaluation of the author's ideas.

It is our hope that these books will give readers a deeper understanding of the issues debated and an appreciation of the complexity of even seemingly simple issues when good and honest people disagree. This awareness is particularly important in a democratic society such as ours in which people enter into public debate to determine the common good. Those with whom one disagrees should not be regarded as enemies but rather as people whose views deserve careful examination and may shed light on one's own.

Thomas Jefferson once said that "difference of opinion leads to inquiry, and inquiry to truth." Jefferson, a broadly educated man, argued that "if a nation expects to be ignorant and free . . . it expects what never was and never will be." As individuals and as a nation, it is imperative that we consider the opinions of others and examine them with skill and discernment. The Opposing Viewpoints Series is intended to help readers achieve this goal.

David L. Bender and Bruno Leone,
Founders

Introduction

"As nervous . . . banks close their doors to growing numbers of would-be borrowers, other sources of credit are booming."

—Russell Lynch,
"Alternative Lenders Profit
as Banks Close Their Doors,"
Daily Post, March 11, 2009.

In the summer of 2007, pundits and financial analysts were abuzz about an impending "credit crunch." Only a year later, headlines seemed to treat the credit crunch as a foregone conclusion. In an article on MSN.com, Jim Jubak described a credit crunch as a circumstance where "lenders stop lending and credit becomes tough to obtain."

Most economists trace the current credit crunch to the subprime mortgage crisis, in which several large mortgage companies gave a high number of loans to high-risk borrowers, those whose income level or credit score would have previously made them unable to get mortgages. To offset their higher risk, mortgage companies generally gave these borrowers "subprime mortgages," which begin with a lower interest rate that later climbs.

In 2007, mortgage companies began seeing high rates of default—borrowers failing to make payments on a loan—largely due to these subprime mortgages. The mortgage industry fell into crisis. American Home Mortgage filed for bankruptcy, Ameriquest went out of business, and Countrywide Financial—the biggest mortgage lender in the United States—only narrowly avoided bankruptcy by taking out an emergency loan. As a result, mortgage companies had less money to lend and more apprehension about lending to risky borrowers. Mortgages became more difficult to obtain, and when they were available, the terms were much stricter.

But the credit crunch didn't stop with the mortgage industry. As Jane J. Kim wrote in the *Wall Street Journal* in August 2007:

> As it gets tougher to land a home loan, some people are also finding it harder and more expensive to get other types of consumer credit.
>
> Some lenders such as USAA [United Services Automobile Association] are nudging up credit score requirements across their auto loans, credit cards and personal loans.

Kim said that the expansion of the credit crunch into other arenas wasn't a direct result of the mortgage crisis, but "reflect[ed] concerns about an economic slowdown and uncertainty about interest rates."

Student loans and small business loans are among the types of lending that have been impacted by the credit crunch. According to Angel Jennings of the *Boston Globe*, "The nation's largest provider of student loans cut the amount of private loans it issues to $7 billion [in 2008], down from $8 billion [in 2007]." An October 2007 survey of senior loan officers by the Federal Reserve found that "nearly one-tenth of responding banks tightened credit standards for small business loans in the third quarter, while none said they had loosened standards."

Unable to obtain loans through traditional means, many consumers have begun turning to alternative lending methods, some old and some new. For instance, Jennings reported that the decline in student loans from traditional lending institutions has had some parents borrowing from their retirement savings or even using credit cards to pay for their children's education. In a 2006 *New York Times* article, Glenn Rifkin told the story of David Ayers, chief executive of Ayer Sales Inc. The business experienced a decline in sales in 2003, and as a result, his bank called in its loan. "Rather than close the business that his father had started in 1961," wrote Rifkin, "Mr. Ayer turned to an alternative that most small business owners prefer to avoid: an asset-based loan from a commercial lender."

At the same time that established forms of alternative lending have grown as a result of the credit crunch, newer forms of alternative lending such as online peer-to-peer lending have taken off. Consumers borrow money from peers, generally over the Internet, and companies such as Prosper or the Lending Club facilitate the transactions, for everything from financing small businesses to paying off credit card debt. John Tozzi wrote in a 2007 *BusinessWeek* article: "Most [peer-to-peer lending] sites reported that between 20 percent to 30 percent of loans are for businesses." In the *Washington Post* in 2008, Michelle Singletary reported, "Javelin [Strategy & Research] predicts that the demand for person-to-person lending services, or P2P, to pay off credit card debt may grow from $38 billion to $159 billion over the next five years."

While the economic landscape has surely changed as a result of the current credit crunch, just how it has changed—and whether these changes are positive or negative, or a little of both—is a matter of debate. The following chapters, "How Does Alternative Lending Compare to Traditional Lending?" "Is Payday Lending a Beneficial Alternative to Traditional Lending?" "Is Peer-to-Peer Lending an Effective Alternative to Traditional Lending?" and "Does Microlending Help the Poor?" examine the positive and negative aspects of various forms of alternative lending. The viewpoints included in these chapters offer a wealth of information that is invaluable for all consumers coping in today's economy.

OPPOSING
VIEWPOINTS®
SERIES

CHAPTER 1

How Does Alternative Lending Compare to Traditional Lending?

Chapter Preface

In the realm of lending and borrowing money, as in other arenas, more opportunity often brings more risk. While the world of alternative lending has broadened in response to the current credit crunch and, thus, presented consumers with more borrowing options, this expanded playing field also requires more caution. Many forms of alternative lending are unregulated or, even if subject to government oversight, carry higher interest rates than traditional lending institutions such as banks. Payday lenders, for example, often charge annualized interest rates of 400 percent or more. Microloans also tend to charge higher interest than bank loans. In a 2006 *Nation* article, Alexander Cockburn wrote, "The interest rates micro-indebted women are paying in India are far higher than commercial bank lending rates," between 24 and 36 percent, while more privileged borrowers pay 6 to 8 percent on a bank loan.

Still, if alternative lenders are the only lenders that will loan money to consumers—especially in a credit crunch—then for some, the higher rates may be worthwhile. As Eric Uhlfelder wrote in a *BusinessWeek* article about microloans, "The rates may not seem onerous to borrowers when their only other source of credit is a loan shark." For many consumers—even in the United States—this is a reality. In a *Dollars & Sense* article in 2006, Howard Karger wrote about the "10 percent of U.S. households—more than 12 million—that have no relationship with a bank, savings institution, credit union, or other mainstream financial service provider." For such people in particular, alternative lending sources are crucial. These people—"the unbanked," as Karger refers to them—have no choice but to accept the higher risks and interest rates that come with many types of alternative lending.

Alternative lending also offers new investment opportunities, for example via such innovations as online peer-to-peer lending. But again, this new opportunity brings with it more risk than traditional forms of investment. In a June 2009 *Sacramento Bee* article, Sarah Frier reported, "Since its inception in 2005, [peer lending site] Prosper.com has had about a 20 percent default rate among its 60,000 loans." In contrast, Invesco reported in January 2009 that the U.S. "bank loan market's default rate currently stands at 4.8 percent."

As Robert H. Frank wrote in a *New York Times* article, "Each society must decide whether the costs of easy credit outweigh the benefits." Frank likens the availability of credit to that of drugs:

> For example, alcoholic beverages, like payday loans, inflict considerable harm on a small percentage of people, but prohibiting alcohol appears to create more serious problems than it solves. Prohibiting cocaine and heroin entails troubling side effects, too. Even so, concern for those most vulnerable to these drugs has led most societies to prohibit them.

In the end, as Frank pointed out, consumers must decide for themselves whether greater access to credit is worth the risks that come with it, an issue explored from many angles by the authors in this chapter. But whatever their conclusion, it is essential that consumers know the details about how alternative lending sources compare to traditional lending sources.

VIEWPOINT

1

> *"Borrowing money from your peers has its perks."*

Nontraditional Lending Offers Viable Alternatives to Traditional Lending

Kathy Chu

In the following viewpoint, USA TODAY personal finance reporter Kathy Chu presents the advantages of alternative lending, in comparison to traditional lending. While there are disadvantages to this type of lending, the benefits Chu identifies include lower interest rates and greater access for those who would not normally qualify for a bank loan. Chu concludes that if alternative lending continues to grow, it will provide yet another benefit to borrowers by encouraging traditional lenders to offer more competitive rates.

As you read, consider the following questions:

1. What are the main reasons borrowers turn to peer-to-peer lenders, according to a survey cited by Kathy Chu?

2. Why does Lending Club try to connect borrowers and lenders with similar interests, according to its founder?

3. As the author relates, why did certain lenders choose to help Liz Rizzo through Zopa?

You list and bid for shoes, concert tickets and even cars online. Why not loans, too?

That's the thought that came to René Clayton last year [2006] when she heard about a Web site that connected consumers who wanted to borrow money with those willing to lend it. She was short on cash and wanted to buy a fence for her yard. But she didn't think she'd be able to take out a bank loan because of her already high debt.

Clayton, of Odessa, Florida, searched online for alternative lenders and found Prosper.com, which facilitates loans among individuals.

"I think it's a really good concept," says Clayton, 40. "People understand this because they're used to eBay and PayPal."

At a time when social networking sites have taken off and trading on eBay has become a national pastime, the idea of borrowing from peers—rather than from banks or credit card companies—is gaining appeal. A handful of companies provide peer-to-peer lending, with each offering its own twist.

Borrowing money from your peers has its perks. You might be able to secure lower rates than what financial institutions charge for unsecured loans. (That said, if you owned a home and could get a home equity loan, you'd probably get a lower rate than you could get borrowing on peer-to-peer sites.)

Not for Everyone

This type of lending isn't for everyone in need of unsecured cash. Most peer-to-peer sites limit the amount you can borrow. And there are generally more borrowers than lenders online, so not every loan will be funded. In addition, those who are more comfortable tapping the generosity of family and friends have little need to seek out these sites.

"There's only so much capital out there," says Jean Garascia, an analyst at Javelin Strategy & Research. "The (online) community is basically calling the shots and figuring out who's going to get loans."

The main reasons why borrowers turn to peer-to-peer lenders? They want to find low interest rates and to avoid piling up credit card debt, according to a November [2007] survey conducted by Javelin.

Some peer-to-peer lenders are more exclusive than others. Virgin Money facilitates loans among family and friends, rather than strangers. Virgin says that avoiding eBay-style loans among strangers allows lenders on its site to feel more comfortable issuing large amounts, such as the down payment on a home.

Lending Club and Zopa offer loans only to those with minimum FICO credit scores [respected estimations developed by Fair Isaac Corporation] of 640. (Scores range from 300 to 850, with 850 being the best.) Even with a good score, though, Lending Club will accept only borrowers with what it regards as manageable debt. The two companies say their policy reduces the risk of default for lenders.

Lending Club also tries to connect borrowers and lenders who have like-minded interests—those from the same school, say, or who work for the same company—to "increase accountability," says Renaud Laplanche, founder and chief executive of Lending Club.

Different Types of Lenders

Prosper is the most laissez-faire of the peer lenders: It allows almost anyone to borrow and lend on its site, after it checks that person's credit and verifies his or her identity. At Prosper, borrowers with the worst credit scores could be stuck with rates as high as 30%, if they're funded at all. Consumers with great credit might be able to receive rates of 7%.

Alternative Loan Sources Are the Best Bet Now

The best place to get a loan right now is the Bank of Grandma. . . . She could lend the money to you and you'd both win: fewer closing costs, you'd pay less than you would to a bank, and she'd earn more. To properly borrow from a relative or friend, use a third party like virginmoney.us to structure it legally. Or use one of the Web's peer-to-peer lending sites such as zopa.com or prosper.com to borrow money in small amounts from other everyday consumers you don't know. So far, they've done a better job than the big boys of keeping their cash flowing.

Linda Stern, "The Credit You Deserve,"
Newsweek, September 29, 2008.

"We think it defeats the purpose if you have to know people" to borrow and lend money, says Chris Larsen, Prosper's CEO [chief executive officer]. "It's kind of like on eBay. If you can only sell products to family and friends, we think that doesn't lead to the best prices."

Zopa, a peer-to-peer lender that started in the U.K. [United Kingdom] and began operating in the United States this month [December 2007], probably has the most unusual model: Borrowers with good credit can get a loan from one of six credit unions that partner with Zopa. And people looking to earn interest on their savings can buy one-year FDIC [Federal Deposit Insurance Corporation]-insured certificates of deposit [CDs] from the credit unions. The CDs pay rates of up to 5.1%.

By buying a CD, lenders can help a borrower—whom they choose based on the person's Zopa profile—reduce payments on a loan. Essentially, the lower the rate the investor accepts on the one-year CD, the more the borrower's payments will be reduced each month.

Peer-to-Peer Lending Is Mutually Beneficial

Liz Rizzo of Los Angeles got an $8,500 loan through Zopa this month to pay off high-rate credit card debt that she says was "killing" her finances. Her loan payment on the three-year loan, at 9.9%, was supposed to be $180.56 a month. But so far, financial help from Zopa members has knocked $4.19 off her monthly loan payments.

Some people chose to help her, rather than other borrowers on the site, Rizzo says, because they identified with her struggle to pay off high-rate credit card debt she'd racked up in grad school.

"People are excited about this concept of helping people while making good money," she says.

Zopa's rates on one-year CDs also compare well with rates available on CDs at conventional financial institutions, making this investment appealing to a broad segment of consumers, not just socially minded people, says Douglas Dolton, Zopa's CEO. Overall, the average rate on a one-year CD is 3.5%, according to Bankrate.com.

For now, peer-to-peer lending makes up only a small slice of overall consumer borrowing. In 2007, an estimated $647 million in peer-to-peer loans will be made, according to Celent, a research firm. This pales when stacked up against the total outstanding consumer debt in the United States of nearly $2.5 trillion.

A Potential Threat to Banks

Yet if demand for peer-to-peer lending continues to ramp up, it could eat into banks' and credit card issuers' market share.

"What you're doing is, you're circumventing financial institutions" by matching borrowers directly to lenders, says

Keith Leggett, a senior economist at the American Bankers Association. "From our standpoint, (this issue) is on our radar screen."

Ultimately, more competition among lenders could benefit a broad range of borrowers. The growth of the market, Leggett says, could be "a potential threat to your unsecured lenders, primarily credit card issuers, (which means) they'll just have to become more competitive" with rates and rewards given to customers.

"When credit markets tighten, structural problems with hedge funds and other alternative lenders will almost certainly worsen the correction that many investors already expect."

Alternative Lending Is Riskier than Traditional Lending

Anthony DiSimone and Jason Perri

In this viewpoint, Anthony DiSimone and Jason Perri argue that the current financial environment of excessive borrowing will eventually lead to a credit crisis. Alternative loans, such as those using hedge funds, have been given to borrowers with default histories. While such loans offer lenders short-term profits, they will inevitably cause a wave of defaults down the road. DiSimone is managing director of Bayside Capital and Perri is an investment professional at Bayside Capital.

As you read, consider the following questions:

1. According to the authors, why are hedge fund loans more attractive to lenders than bank loans?

2. Which structural aspects of alternative asset funds will amplify the bursting of the credit bubble, in the authors' opinion?

3. In what way does the savings and loan crisis of the 1980s provide a useful example, according to Anthony DiSimone and Jason Perri?

Looking to put money to work in a crowded marketplace, hedge funds, bulge bracket investment banks, CLO/CDO [collateralized loan obligation/collateralized debt obligation] funds and private equity firms have all entered the loan origination business in recent years. The resulting surge in available debt capital has driven aggressive borrowing to finance leveraged buyouts and M&A [mergers and acquisitions] activity, as well as to refinance existing indebtedness with cheaper, less restrictive loans. This easy refinancing environment has allowed issuers who would have defaulted to borrow and avoid default without necessarily fixing their underlying financial problems. Moreover, many funds are not ideally suited or structured to operate as lenders, and when credit markets tighten, structural problems with hedge funds and other alternative lenders will almost certainly worsen the correction that many investors already expect.

In [the] first three quarters of 2006 alone, U.S. companies have borrowed over $525 billion, a 29% increase from last year's [2005] $409 billion for the same period, according to Thomson Financial. The number of new issues also continued to rise, to 1,554 so far in 2006, up from 1,380 a year ago.

Even stressed companies have enjoyed a seemingly limitless refinancing market that has forestalled the onset of true financial distress in many situations. This phenomenon has driven default rates to historical lows. In the U.S. leveraged loan market, default rates declined to 1.2% in September [2006], the lowest level since April 2005, as reported by Standard & Poor's [S&P]. By comparison, the average default rate from 1985 to 2005 was 4.9% and at its peak in 2002 topped 14%, according to Edward Altman, professor of finance at New York University.

Clearly the rise in leveraged loan volumes, even at current default rates, will lead to a proportional increase in the volume of distressed debt over time—an outcome the distressed investing community has been expecting for years. And while the timing of a correction is difficult to predict, the specific drivers of the coming default wave that relate to alternative lenders are particularly worrisome.

The Allure of Alternative Loans

Seeking a share of the lucrative fees and higher rates offered by leveraged loans, and in search of ways to deploy vast amounts of cash at their disposal, fund managers have been fielding dedicated teams to analyze and execute opportunities to originate structured loans. Over the last five years [2002–2006], the ranks of hedge funds specializing in credit strategies have swelled from just a handful to more than 400. In fact, hedge funds alone now represent over one-third of available leveraged loan capital, according to Greenwich Associates.

Eschewing traditional "bank" credit hierarchies, funds often have centralized portfolio control and can make rapid decisions on structure, rates and covenants. Moreover, hedge fund managers accustomed to greater levels of risk are willing to accept significantly higher leverage multiples and less downside protection than typical bank lenders in exchange for lower volatility than the public high yield markets. Not surprisingly, such loans present an attractive alternative for financial sponsors seeking to finance deals in as efficient and profit-maximizing a manner as possible.

Those features of alternative loans are even more tempting to stressed firms facing liquidity crises and in search of rapid rescue financings with loose terms. And as more capital has crowded the playing field, funds have increasingly been lend-

The Credit Crunch to Come

For the last three years, deal makers have been riding a wave of liquidity [ease in converting assets to cash] that made financing acquisitions the least of their worries. While deals faced other hurdles during this period, it was a rare transaction that floundered because buyers couldn't arrange financing.

"It's been an extraordinarily benign lending environment. Buyers have had access to cheap money and lenders have been increasingly tolerant," says David Stowell, a finance professor at Northwestern University's Kellogg School of Management.

But just as every party has to end, experts say, a credit crunch is on the way. . . .

When the squeeze comes, deal makers expect a slowdown in deal flow, lower prices, increased difficulties for private equity players to exit their holdings, and an edge to well-heeled strategic buyers, as well as more contentious workouts for those companies that get into trouble. Some deal and debt pros who already are hunkering down suggest that buyers get more choosy about pricing, craft more flexible and less burdensome deal structures, and select lenders that are most likely to be understanding in a pinch. A reverse tide to traditional banks from hard-nosed alternative lenders is a strong possibility.

Brent Shearer,
"Battening Down for a Credit Crunch,"
Mergers and Acquisitions Journal, *August 1, 2006.*

ing to these credits. To make such loans possible, lenders have been extending more leverage with less covenant restriction on borrower financial performance—an obviously risky combination. Total leverage versus last year has been almost half of a turn of earnings higher, at an average of 5.5x to 6.0x EBITDA [earnings before interest, taxes, depreciation, and amortization]. In addition, for noninvestment grade loans in the first half of 2006, the occurrence of a coverage covenant of any type dropped to 61%, a significant decline from 70% in 2005 and the 1996–2005 average of 78%. In sharp contrast, leverage multiples in the years preceding 2002, the year in which default rates hit their 14% peak, were in the 3.5x to 4.5x range, according to S&P.

Expediting the Bubble Burst

In past credit cycles large lending institutions with diversified balance sheets and highly structured workout processes helped soften the blow of heavier default activity, even if their overextension was responsible for an overheated market. In contrast, certain structural aspects of alternative asset funds may in fact magnify the speed and severity of the bursting of the current credit bubble.

First, most hedge funds have a shorter-term investment horizon and have neither the inclination nor the resources for a lengthy troubled loan workout. While many veteran distressed fund managers have expertise in navigating creditor committees and protecting their investments in bankruptcy cases, far fewer managers in the larger community of funds have the appetite for the time, expense and uncertainty inherent in a restructuring.

Second, hedge funds have a short-term incentive structure. Most funds measure returns and distribute carry on a quarterly basis. Managers can thus improve current returns by generating fees and high call premia on the front end of a loan regardless of the risk of default on the back end, which is often years away.

Finally, there is an obvious duration mismatch between most alternative lending funds and the loans they originate. Most funds have shorter-term lockups while leveraged loans tend to be long-term, illiquid liabilities [not readily converted to cash]. Funds facing investor calls cannot normally demand a return of capital from their borrowers in order to satisfy liquidity needs. Usually the only alternative for a manager in such a situation is to sell an entire portfolio when one or two bad loans precipitate unexpected redemptions.

Damage Control

The good news is that more hedge funds and private equity firms stand to benefit from the coming correction than are at risk from it. The aftermath of the savings and loan [S&L] meltdown in the late 1980s provides an analogous and instructive example to predict the potential outcome for many troubled loans when the current cycle turns. Then, private equity and real estate firms with longer-term, control-oriented investment strategies (as opposed to traditional lending institutions) stepped in and provided liquidity in the real estate market by purchasing distressed loans from the Resolution Trust Corporation [RTC].

Most such firms had experience in owning and managing properties and were able to assemble robust portfolios at modest valuations. In today's market, distressed and special situations funds with longer investment horizons and experience as equity holders will similarly provide liquidity to companies that levered excessively or irresponsibly simply because the capital was available. The existence of such investors and their early willingness to assist alternative lenders in monetizing troublesome positions should prevent a shakeout as extreme as in the S&L crisis. The rationalization of the credit overhang will be a powerful reminder, though, that debt that looks like equity often will become equity sooner or later.

| "Many newer mortgage products make it difficult and costly for borrowers . . . to extricate themselves."

Alternative Mortgage Loans Are Riskier than Traditional Mortgages

Kirstin Downey

Kirstin Downey, a business writer for the Washington Post *from 1988–2008, is the author of* The Woman Behind the New Deal: The Life of Frances Perkins, FDR's Secretary of Labor and His Moral Conscience. *In the following viewpoint, Downey reports that alternative mortgage loans originally intended for a specific, market-savvy class of people, are now being aggressively promoted to the larger public. Many homeowners agree to nontraditional mortgages without fully understanding how they work, and end up unable to afford the interest rates. While in the past, these consumers could have sold their homes before defaulting on their mortgages, the tightness of the current housing market often precludes this possibility.*

As you read, consider the following questions:

1. According to the author, what kind of down payment is usually required for traditional fixed-rate mortgages?

2. How do subprime mortgage loans differ from traditional mortgage loans, according to Kirstin Downey?

3. According to the viewpoint, how has the market changed to make riskier loans more attractive to lenders?

At 64, and looking toward his retirement next year, Willie Lee Howard agreed to refinance his duplex in Northeast Washington, thinking that a fixed-rate loan would help stabilize his finances.

What Howard got instead was a mortgage he did not understand. Baffled by the loan documents he was mailed after the closing, he consulted an AARP [a membership organization for people 50 and older] lawyer and learned that he now had an interest-only loan, a new and controversial kind of mortgage. Howard was told that under its terms, his mortgage balance will rise instead of fall and that he will need to refinance in 10 years, when he may be too old to work.

"This is a bunch of junk they done to me," said Howard, a construction worker.

Howard's chagrin at his mortgage's complex provisions illustrates the confusion felt by many borrowers struggling to adapt to a radically transformed home lending market. Consumer advocates say most people learned about mortgages from their parents and grandparents, who typically put down 20 percent on a 30-year fixed loan on which they always knew what their payments would be.

Those long-standing assumptions have been challenged in recent years by the rapid proliferation of new loan products with looser credit requirements and fluctuating payment plans. Although the newer mortgage products allow almost anyone to buy or refinance a house, consumer groups say the loans often contain land mines hidden in the fine print.

Consumer advocates say the loosened standards are putting more people at risk as loans originally designed for sophisticated individuals are being marketed to far-less-savvy borrowers.

"Consumers haven't caught up with the dynamics of the market," said Allen J. Fishbein, director of housing and credit policy at the Consumer Federation of America. "They are still thinking of how it used to be, but it isn't like that anymore."

Product Comparison

Alternative mortgage loans were first developed for a handful of people with promising long-term earnings potential: young lawyers destined to make partner, doctors finishing medical school, or stockbrokers who get large commission checks several times a year.

But as housing prices have surged, outstripping wages in the most expensive markets, alternative financing has become a popular path to homeownership.

These new loans come in many forms. "Nontraditional" mortgages allow borrowers to pay only the interest on the loan or even only a portion of the interest each month, without being required to pay down the principal. Nationwide, more than a third of borrowers who got loans in the first nine months of 2006 got nontraditional loans, up from about 2 percent in 2000, according to First American LoanPerformance, a real estate information firm.

"Piggyback" loans allow people to borrow for a down payment, sparing buyers the trouble of saving for years and letting them avoid paying mortgage insurance, which is usually required on loans with down payments of less than 20 percent. In 2005, about 22 percent of people buying homes took out piggyback mortgages, according to the Federal Reserve.

"Subprime" loans are available to people who have bad credit, though they charge interest rates 2 to 3 percent higher than the rates charged to borrowers with good credit. About a fifth of the loans originated in 2006 now fall into that category, up from about 5 percent in 1999, according to the Federal Reserve.

New Opportunities Come with New Risks

Jim Sugarman, supervisory attorney at AARP's financial-abuse unit, says these alternative loans offer new opportunities but also carry added risks. About 59 percent of subprime loans have adjustable rates, according to the Mortgage Bankers Association, and any sudden spike in interest rates would push payments higher.

In a rising real estate market like that of the past few years, borrowers who fall behind on their mortgages could sell before going into default. For that reason, lenders haven't been too worried about repayment. But now, with home prices flat or falling, many homeowners may not be able to sell their homes for enough to cover their mortgage balances.

Alternative loan products are giving many people access to homeownership, counters Steve Calem, vice president with American Bank in Bethesda [Maryland]. "Interest-only loans help people get into their first house," he said. "Interest-only loans minimize their payments, when people know their income is going to be going up. It gives them flexibility."

Most consumers have only themselves to blame because they are not doing enough research on the mortgage market as it has grown increasingly complex, said Christopher Cruise, who trains mortgage brokers at major lending companies.

"The American consumer's ignorance of mortgage procedures in the past hurt them a little," he said. "What's different now is that it'll hurt them a lot. The stakes are a lot higher."

Persistent Phone Calls

Howard said he was persuaded to refinance his house by a "very friendly" loan officer who called once a week for a year, telling him the time was right to stabilize his finances.

After deciding to take out the loan, he said he told the lender he would need help reading the paperwork at the closing. He said he still doesn't understand exactly what kind of mortgage he signed.

Howard's mortgage contains several of these new features, said Sugarman, who has reviewed the documents. It is an interest-only loan, which is one of the nontraditional mortgages designed to help wealthy people manage their cash flow, and for people whose incomes are likely to rise—not for those whose incomes such as Howard's are likely to fall as they retire on Social Security. The rate is fixed, but only for 10 years. Sugarman said Howard appears to have qualified for it with a "NINA" loan, a "no-income, no assets" loan that required minimal income documentation.

"It's a very exotic mortgage, and he had no idea he was getting that," Sugarman said. "He thought he was doing something smart."

Market Shifts

Sugarman said that in the past, lenders didn't make these kinds of loans because they put financial institutions at risk. Bad real estate loans marked the beginning of the Great Depression, and subsequent banking reforms required lenders to consider the soundness of their lending practices. That made loans safer for borrowers and lenders alike.

What has changed is the booming market for real estate securities? Major financial institutions now put thousands of loans together and sell them in slices to investors. That means lenders seldom get caught holding the loans. If an individual loan goes bad, the effect is dissipated among many investors.

Nontraditional Mortgages Have Higher Delinquency Rates

Record numbers of people have taken out nontraditional mortgages, loans with lower initial payments or other options designed to help buyers with limited resources overcome skyrocketing home prices.

But these loans—which in some cases are considered predatory by consumer advocates—come with higher risks. . . .

Comprising less than 1 percent of the loan market in 2000, some estimate that as many as a third of all mortgages currently are nontraditional loans, Allen J. Fishbein, director of housing and credit policy for the Consumer Federation of America, testified before the Senate [Committee on] Banking, Housing, and Urban Affairs . . . in September [2006]. . . .

Rebecca Boreczky,
"Nontraditional Loans Can Carry Big Risks,"
Washington Times, *November 17, 2006.*

The new mortgage products have fueled record profits for the lending industry in recent years. Brokers can generate tens of thousands of dollars in additional fees, beyond what they earn on traditional mortgages, by placing borrowers in these loans, Cruise said.

The question is whether some consumers can adequately protect themselves in the complex financial transactions of the new mortgage marketplace.

A Tough Price to Pay

Willie Webb Jr. of Lauderdale Lakes, Fla., was pleased for his daughter at first when she told him she had refinanced the home she had inherited from her grandparents, reducing her interest rate and allowing her to pay off some bills. He assumed she had gotten a fixed-rate mortgage, the kind of loan with which he is most familiar. A few months later, she called him in a panic. It turned out that she had an adjustable-rate mortgage in which the payments starting rising almost immediately, and when Webb investigated further, he learned that she can't get out of the loan without paying a $6,000 prepayment penalty.

Webb is angry that his daughter, Keisha Smith, a single mother with four children, agreed to take a loan she did not understand. He has made the payments for her some months because otherwise she would risk losing her home.

Many newer mortgage products make it difficult and costly for borrowers like Smith to extricate themselves. The Mortgage Bankers Group recently reported that more than 50 percent of some kinds of adjustable-rate loans contain prepayment penalties, which require borrowers to shell out big bucks to break free. A prepayment penalty of about 3 percent of the mortgage loan—about $9,000 on a $300,000 mortgage—is not unusual, according to the Federal Reserve.

A study by the Center for Responsible Lending, a consumer-advocacy group, said last year that about two-thirds of Virginians with high-interest, subprime loans also have prepayment penalties. In Maryland, where prepayment penalties are restricted by law, about a quarter of subprime borrowers have them. (Comparable figures were not available for the District [of Columbia].)

Mitigating Risks

The biggest risk lurking behind all these loans is the threat of foreclosure. Last month [December 2006], the Mortgage Bankers Association reported that mortgage delinquencies were on the rise, particularly for costly subprime loans. Likewise, the Center for Responsible Lending said in a recent report that more than 19 percent of subprime loans made in 2005 and 2006 are at risk of foreclosure.

Federal and state banking regulators have instructed lenders to make sure before issuing a loan that borrowers can keep up if payments are adjusted upward. Consumer advocates and some members of Congress have asked that the guidance also include what is called a 2/28 mortgage, under which borrowers have low, teaser rates during the first two years, after which payments increase.

Consumer groups also say they would like to see a "suitability" standard imposed on mortgages whereby lenders would be required to show that people got loans appropriate for them. Sugarman, for example, thinks putting Howard into an interest-only loan left the man with a "horrible situation." But banking trade groups oppose these proposals, saying they could curtail lending to some people who would otherwise have trouble getting loans they need.

Additional government regulation "could impede the ability of the market" to change to meet demand, said Doug Duncan, the chief economist at the Mortgage Bankers Association.

But Fishbein, the consumer activist, said legislators, regulators, and lenders need to do more to protect consumers.

"We're not confident buyers are getting all the information they need," he said. "They don't understand the toxic environment."

> *"These Americans can become bank customers if they have access to the right products at the right terms, and the support they need to make good, responsible financial decisions."*

Traditional Lending Should Be as Accessible as Alternative Lending

William J. Clinton and Arnold Schwarzenegger

In this viewpoint, William J. (Bill) Clinton, former president of the United States, and Arnold Schwarzenegger, governor of California, discuss "unbanked" Americans. Either because of distrust or a lack of access, some Americans do not utilize banks and are dependent on alternative lenders, many of whom exploit their customers' vulnerability with high fees and interest rates. The authors argue in support of initiatives such as the one launched in California that help unbanked residents open starter bank accounts. Such projects, they say, would put more than $8 billion a year back into the American economy and the pockets of working Americans, rather than exploitative lenders.

As you read, consider the following questions:

1. According to the authors, how do payday loan fees compare to the average credit card rate?

2. What percentage of California households do not have a checking account, according to the article?

3. In the authors' view, how can banks and credit unions help those not already benefitting from their services?

The American dream is founded on the belief that people who work hard and play by the rules will be able to earn a good living, raise a family in comfort, and retire with dignity.

But that dream is harder to achieve for millions of Americans because they spend too much of their hard-earned money on fees to cash their paychecks or pay off high-priced loans meant to carry them over until they get paid at work.

Here is one initiative that can unite progressives and conservatives as well as business leaders and community activists: helping the "unbanked" enter the financial mainstream by opening checking and savings accounts, and working collaboratively with financial institutions and community groups to develop and market products that work for this untapped market. This will put money in the pockets of individuals and grow the economy. And it won't cost taxpayers a dime.

Imagine the economic and social benefits of putting more than $8 billion in the hands of low- and middle-income Americans. That is the amount millions of people now spend each year at check-cashing outlets, payday lenders, and pawnshops on basic financial services that most Americans receive for free—or very little cost—at their local bank or credit union. Over a lifetime, the average full-time, unbanked worker will spend more than $40,000 just to turn his or her salary into cash.

It Is Expensive to Be Unbanked

Maria Guzman and her family are part of the 10% of U.S. households—more than 12 million—that have no relationship with a bank, savings institution, credit union, or other mainstream financial service provider. Being "unbanked," the Guzmans turn to the fringe economy for check cashing, bill payment, short-term pawn or payday loans, furniture and appliance rentals, and a host of other financial services. In each case, they face high user fees and exorbitant interest rates.

Without credit, the Guzmans must buy a car either for cash or through a "buy-here/pay-here" (BHPH) used car lot. At a BHPH lot they are saddled with a 28% annual percentage rate (APR) on a high-mileage and grossly overpriced vehicle. They also pay weekly, and one missed payment means a repossession. Since the Guzmans have no checking account, they use a check casher who charges 2.7% for cashing their monthly $1,500 in payroll checks, which costs them $40.50 a month or $486 a year. . . .

Howard Karger,
"America's Growing Fringe Economy,"
Dollars & Sense, *November-December 2006.*

A Ready-Made Market

Many nonbank customers are either leery of banks or believe they do not have the products they need. The result is that the market for basic financial services is booming. Today, the number of check cashers, payday lenders, and pawnshops is more than double the number of McDonald's franchises in the United States. More than 20 million Americans cash more than $60 billion in checks each year at check-cashing businesses. Full-time workers without a checking account typically pay $40 on average to cash their paychecks. And payday lenders sell an additional $40 billion in expensive small-dollar loans each year that carry fees 30 times the average credit card rate.

But these Americans can become bank customers if they have access to the right products at the right terms, and the support they need to make good, responsible financial decisions. People outside of the financial mainstream are the heart of America. The vast majority of people without bank accounts work, and they have an average household income of $27,000. Most are also married, have at least one child, and are employed by a small business.

And consider that, according to a new Brookings Institution report, as much as $360,000 in pre-tax wealth could be created if the average, full-time unbanked worker invested in the stock market what he will spend over his lifetime paying to cash his paychecks. That would allow one of those workers to finance about 25 years of retirement at his current standard of living.

Support Is Building

This year [2008], California will become the first state in the nation to launch an effort to help unbanked residents open starter accounts—the first step into the financial mainstream. Approximately 11% of California households, including 25% of Latino and African American households, do not have a checking account. And nearly half of households in the state don't have a savings account.

In coordination with the Federal Deposit Insurance Corporation [FDIC], we will partner with financial institutions to increase the supply of starter accounts that work for unbanked consumers and banks. We will form regional coalitions of financial institutions, mayors and community groups to market accounts and help the unbanked build financial literacy. And we will build on work already being done in San Francisco, where city officials, working with banks and credit unions, have already signed up 11,000 individuals who previously had no checking or savings account.

The William J. Clinton Foundation's Economic Opportunity Initiative will help more people enter the financial mainstream by supporting the work of California—as well as that of mayors in Boston, Los Angeles, Miami, New York, Providence, San Francisco, Savannah, and Seattle, each of whom are spearheading their own efforts. It will also work to engage additional cities and states, and the private sector.

Further Help Is Needed

We need other leaders across the country in the public, private, and nonprofit sectors to join this effort. Banks and credit unions can expand their efforts to broaden access to transaction accounts and alternatives to payday loans with terms attractive to the unbanked and underserved. They already have the storefronts to compete for this business: More than 90% of nonbank alternatives are located within one mile of a bank or credit union branch.

Employers can also help reduce the financial stress in workers' lives and boost workplace morale by helping employees to gain access to banking services, and to save and better manage their finances. Community-based organizations can work with the public and private sectors to help people access the trustworthy, high-quality money management support they may need to develop and sustain good personal financial practices.

By working together, we can improve the lives of millions of people, boost our economy, and strengthen our communities.

Periodical Bibliography

The following articles have been selected to supplement the diverse views presented in this chapter.

Zoran Basich	"Lending, with a Twist," *Wall Street Journal*, October 13, 2008.
Boston Globe	"Exotic Loans Carry Big Risks," December 31, 2006.
Harold Brubaker	"Businesses Turn to Alternative Lending," *Philadelphia Inquirer*, January 29, 2009.
Economist	"Into the Fold: Americans Without Bank Accounts," May 6, 2006.
Tim Grant	"The Credit Crunch: How Did It Happen and Where Do We Go from Here?" *Pittsburgh Post-Gazette*, December 23, 2007.
Annette Haddad	"Risky 'Exotic' Loans Fostering a Refi Cycle," *Los Angeles Times*, October 10, 2005.
Barbara Kiviat	"The Credit Crunch: Where Is It Happening," *TIME*, September 30, 2008.
Elaine Pofeldt	"Tips for Finding Financing When Banks Say No," *Crain's New York Business*, July 13, 2009.
Peter Schworm	"College Loans See Subprime Fallout," *Boston Globe*, March 7, 2008.
Brian Truscott	"An Alternative Lending Model, Without the Subprime Headache," *Toronto Star*, October 25, 2007.

CHAPTER 2

Is Payday Lending a Beneficial Alternative to Traditional Lending?

Chapter Preface

With the abundance of payday lending businesses in every corner of America, it's hard to believe this industry is a relatively new one. In fact, as Daniel Brook reported in his 2009 *Harper's* article, there were fewer than two hundred payday lending stores in the United States in the early 1990s. "Today," he said, "there are over twenty-two thousand, serving 10 million households each year—a $40 billion industry with more U.S. locations, in fact, than McDonald's." In contrast, Robert H. Frank wrote in the *New York Times* that industry revenue reached less than $1 billion in 1998.

What conditions have created the market for this kind of service? Surprisingly, the bulk of payday lending customers are not the lowest income Americans. In fact, the assertion by the payday lending industry's trade group, the Community Financial Services Association of America, that "Payday advance customers represent the heart of America's middle class" is fairly accurate and, as Frank said, "testifies to the financial instability of all but the most affluent Americans." Most economists agree that wages in the United States have not kept up with inflation—some say that when adjusted for inflation, the current minimum wage is lower than the 1968 level. As a result, as Frank wrote, "Fully 47 percent of Americans now report living paycheck to paycheck." And, for the first time since the Great Depression, the personal savings rate of Americans reached negative levels in 2005, falling as low as—0.5 percent, according to Tom Abate of the *San Francisco Chronicle*. This circumstance provides ample opportunity for payday lenders. When wages are just enough to cover everyday expenses, and an unexpected expense comes up—a health crisis, a car breaking down, and so on—consumers with no savings have no choice but to borrow money to meet these expenses.

Some critics believe payday lenders wrongly exploit borrowers in such desperate circumstances, charging exorbitant interest rates because they know borrowers have no other choice. Many of these critics promote active government regulation of these lenders, such as interest rate limits—or outright prohibition, which has taken place in a number of states already. But others argue that the payday lending industry offers a valuable service, access to money that borrowers need and wouldn't otherwise be able to obtain. These commentators believe consumers should be given the choice whether to take out loans or not, assuming they are fully informed of the provisions of the loan. The ethics of payday lending is among the many debates surrounding this industry and among the issues explored by the authors in the following chapter. In the current economic climate, when American consumer debt is at an all-time high, it is essential that Americans be informed of the implications of borrowing from alternative loan sources such as payday lenders.

"Contrary to the fears of the credit snobs, the readier access to credit . . . [does] not tempt the new customers into a debt trap."

Payday Lending Provides Opportunities for Borrowers

Economist

In the following viewpoint, the Economist *disputes claims that profiting from the poor, as payday lenders do, is implicitly immoral. Such arguments insult the poor by assuming they are incapable of looking out for their own interests. The author discusses a study of for-profit lenders in several poor neighborhoods in South Africa. Instead of being trapped in a debt cycle, the borrowers thrived with the new credit; they were more likely to keep their jobs because they had the financial resources to overcome unforeseen obstacles and even invest in resources that made it easier to get to their jobs.*

As you read, consider the following questions:

1. According to the author, why do critics of for-profit lending believe it is wrong to profit from the poor?

"In Praise of Usury," *Economist*, vol. 384, August 4, 2007, p. 66. © The Economist Newspaper Limited, London 2007. All rights reserved. Republished with permission of The Economist, conveyed through Copyright Clearance Center, Inc.

2. Why have some governments put strict regulations on consumer lending, according to the article?

3. Why might South African borrowers feel more positive and in control of their lives with more access to credit, in the author's estimation?

In [Italian poet] Dante's *Divine Comedy*, [a view of the Christian afterlife] usurers are consigned to a flaming desert of sand within the seventh circle of hell. Attitudes have since softened a bit. Microcreditors, who offer small loans to self-employed poor people, enjoy hallowed reputations. One has even ascended to the rank of a Nobel laureate. But lending to the poor is still considered distasteful whenever it is pricey, short-term and profitable. In America, for example, many activists are quick to damn "payday" lenders, who may charge high fees for offering cash advances on a worker's next pay cheque.

Why this hostility? To profit from lending to the poor, critics say, is to prey on the most vulnerable, at their most vulnerable moment. Faced with desperate customers, loan sharks can charge well over the odds, even when the risk of default is slight. The money they proffer is often squandered on spurious consumption, critics say, rather than productive investments that would help the borrower repay his debts. Easy credit thus tempts people into a damaging spiral of indebtedness.

That may be enough for Dante. But economists take a bit more convincing. If loans hurt the poor, why do they take them? Surely they are capable of looking after their own interests. Alex Tabarrok, an influential economics blogger, thinks the anti-usury lobby are "credit snobs", who think that credit is something only the rich can handle.

Protecting People from Themselves?

Some critics of usury appeal to psychology not snobbery, however. The "behavioural" economists have shown that people's decisions often conflict with the plans they had laid for themselves. When planning for the future, people are willing to defer gratification, forgoing smaller, earlier rewards in favour of bigger, later ones. But when choosing in the present, they give up huge future benefits for immediate gratification. If they anticipate their own weakness, people may quite rationally chop up their credit cards, or tie money up in illiquid [not easily converted to cash] assets. It is the financial equivalent of avoiding restaurants with irresistible desserts.

Some governments have concluded that by denying expensive credit to the poor, they would be doing them a favour. In America, many states have crimped payday lending by imposing anti-usury laws or restrictions on lending terms. In Japan, interest-rate caps have, in effect, wiped out much of the formal consumer-lending industry.

In poorer countries, governments are ambivalent. On the one hand, they are anxious to subsidise microfinance, extending small-business loans further than the market allows. But they take the opposite attitude towards consumer credit, imposing interest-rate caps that stop lenders reaching as many people as they otherwise might. South Africa this year [2007] tightened curbs on reckless lending and overborrowing.

Widening the Circle

Is the South African government right to think that credit has gone too far? Rather than relying on theology or theory to answer this question, a recent working paper offers some rare evidence. Dean Karlan, a Yale economist who is codirector of the Financial Access Initiative, and Jonathan Zinman, of Dartmouth College, studied a profit-seeking lender that served some of South Africa's poorer neighbourhoods. Suspecting that its credit standards were too strict, the lender was willing to experiment with a looser provision of credit. It asked its loan officers in Cape Town, Port Elizabeth, and Durban to reconsider 325 out of 787 applicants who had narrowly missed

> ## Payday Loans Are Often Better than Competing Options
>
> Anti-payday politicians such as erstwhile Democratic presidential candidate John Edwards say that these loans are "predatory" and take advantage of desperate borrowers. But the alternatives—such as bank "overdraft" fees for bounced checks and late payment charges on utility bills—can be even costlier. . . .
>
> Evidence is already mounting . . . that caps on payday loans reduce choices for consumers and leave them financially worse off than before.
>
> *John Berlau, "Keep Virginia Market Free,"*
> Washington Times, *February 3, 2008.*

out on approval for a loan. The lucky 325 were chosen at random—nothing distinguished them from the remaining 462, except the luck of the draw. This allowed the researchers to establish a causal link between the loan and changes in the lives of the applicants.

Most of the new customers took a four-month loan at an annual interest rate of about 200%: A 1,000-rand [South African currency unit] loan, for example, would be repaid in four monthly instalments of 367.50 rand. For the bank, the study proved the wisdom of stretching its lending limits. The new clients were profitable, if not as profitable as the borrowers already on their books. The authors reckon the bank made a gain of at least 201 rand per loan.

Credit Helps the Poor Prosper

Did these profits come at the expense of the poor? On the contrary. Despite the demanding terms on offer, those reconsidered for a loan seemed to prosper. Six to twelve months later, they were less likely to go hungry, and their chances of being in poverty fell by 19%. Not coincidentally, they were also more likely to have kept their jobs, perhaps because the credit helped them to overcome emergencies that might otherwise have forced them to abandon their posts. About a fifth of them, for example, spent their loan on transport such as buying or repairing a car that they might have needed to get to work.

The results were not all as happy: The authors found some evidence of higher stress, especially among female borrowers. But people also reported more control over their lives and a more positive outlook. Perhaps the easier access to credit allowed them to take a longer-term perspective, even if "longer term" is measured in months or weeks rather than the more conventional notion of decades.

Contrary to the fears of the credit snobs, the readier access to credit did not tempt the new customers into a debt trap. Over 15–27 months, those reconsidered for a loan were more likely to have a formal credit score. And this score suffered no harm as a result of their easier borrowing.

Overall, the study suggests that profit-seeking lenders do not deserve the fate Dante reserved for them. Far from tempting the poor into unpayable debt, they help them keep their jobs, put food on the table, and build up a credit history. The authors show that poor people can make good use of borrowed money, even if they sometimes struggle to demonstrate this creditworthiness to lenders. If not hell, that is a kind of purgatory.

> *"Payday loans carry annual interest rates of 400 percent and are designed to catch working people ... in a long-term debt trap."*

Payday Lending Traps Borrowers in a Cycle of Debt

Center for Responsible Lending

The Center for Responsible Lending (CRL) is a research and policy organization focused on eradicating exploitative financial practices. In this viewpoint, CRL argues that payday loans are designed to catch borrowers in a cycle of ongoing debt. Such loans carry exorbitant interest rates, often making it impossible for borrowers to pay off past loans without taking out new loans. CRL disputes claims made by the payday lending industry that payday loans are a less costly alternative to bank overdraft fees. In reality, one is rarely used in place of the other. Furthermore, one report found that payday loans actually increase overdrafts.

As you read, consider the following questions:

1. According to the article, what is the cause of most overdrafts?

Center for Responsible Lending, "Payday Loans Put Families in the Red," CRL Issue Brief, February 2009. Copyright © 2009 Center for Responsible Lending. Reproduced by permission.

2. How many payday borrowers default on their loans within a year, according to CRL?

3. In the opinion of CRL, what is the only legal measure that has effectively regulated payday lending?

Marketed as short-term relief for a cash crunch, payday loans carry annual interest rates of 400 percent and are designed to catch working people—or those with a steady source of income such as Social Security or a disability check—in a long-term debt trap.

The terms are set so that borrowers most often cannot pay off the loan on payday when it's due without leaving a large gap in their budget, often forcing them to immediately take out a new loan after paying the first one back. One recent study found that people who took out payday loans nearly doubled their chances of filing for bankruptcy. These households' higher bankruptcy risk exists even when compared to households with similar financial status who were denied a payday loan.

Overdraft fees burden the same people: those living paycheck-to-paycheck. Banks and credit unions routinely approve uncovered transactions without warning their customers of a negative account balance, and charge an average $34 fee for each incident, even when the uncovered purchase amounts to just a few dollars.

Payday lenders argue that working people are better off getting a payday loan than overdrawing their account, and claim that meaningful curbs on abusive payday lending, such as a 36% rate cap, will only increase the number of overdrafts incurred by cash-strapped families. This does not bear out— payday loans and overdrafts are not substitutes for each other. Rather, as shown in a University of North Carolina study of low- and moderate-income families—and the industry's own surveys—payday borrowers tend to have a variety of options besides taking a payday loan or recurring an overdraft fee.

How Payday Loans Snowball

The biggest problem, consumer advocates say, and the biggest source of profits to lenders, is that too many customers find . . . that they must "roll over" the loans, repaying the same fee each month until they can muster the original loan amount.

Over several months, they can easily spend far more on fees than they ever received in cash and may end up by borrowing from multiple sites to pay off others.

One restaurant cashier, . . . Pat T., a 39-year-old mother of five who did not want to embarrass her family by giving her full name, said she had borrowed $200 last year when she could not pay an electric bill because "it was so easy to do." It took her six months to repay the $200, and by then, she had paid $510 in fees.

Erik Eckholm,
"Seductively Easy, Payday Loans Often Snowball,"
New York Times, *December 23, 2006.*

The Truth About Overdrafts

In reality, most overdrafts are accidentally caused by small debit card purchases of about $20, not larger checks which might be used to pay an important bill. Very few bank customers knowingly overdraw their account—in a 2006 CRL survey, only five percent of account holders reported ever using their debit card or writing a check when they knew there were not enough funds in their account to cover the transaction.

Additionally, a new study by Bretton Woods, a private consulting firm which lists the payday lenders' trade association as a client, shows no evidence that households in states without payday lending incur greater overdraft or NSF [non-sufficient funds] fees than households in other states. For example, two-thirds of the states without payday lending pay less than the national average in overdraft/NSF fees, and the share of household income spent on overdraft/NSF fees is the same or greater in states with payday lending, as compared to states without the product.

Not surprisingly, because payday loans are secured by a borrower's personal check or automatic electronic access to a borrower's bank, much of the available data suggest that payday lending may actually *increase* involuntary bank fees. Because one-quarter to half of all payday borrowers default in a twelve-month period, payday lending can actually spur overdraft fees.

In North Carolina, payday borrowers paid over $2 million in NSF fees to payday lenders in addition to the fees assessed by their banks in the last year their practice was legal. Moreover, a new report from Harvard Business School researchers finds that payday lending can increase the odds that households will repeatedly overdraft and ultimately have their banks close their checking accounts. Therefore, rather than lessening the impact of overdraft fees on a family's budget, payday lending can actually increase them.

More Federal Regulation Is Needed

Federal regulators and policy makers have recently turned their attention toward overdraft fee regulation. The GAO [Government Accountability Office] and FDIC [Federal Deposit Insurance Corporation] have documented bank and credit union overdraft practices, and the Federal Reserve has proposed rules that would take steps toward reform. Federal legislation has also been proposed that would require that account holders have a clear understanding of the cost of overdraft programs, and that would prohibit banks from engaging in unfair practices such as clearing the day's transactions from the highest to the lowest in order to increase the number of fees they can charge.

A 36 percent interest rate cap for high-cost loans eliminates the predatory practice of charging 400 percent for loans to working people and will reduce the bank fees unnecessarily assessed because of faulty payday loans. A two-digit interest rate cap is already saving 15 states and the District of Columbia nearly $1.8 billion in predatory payday fees alone, and a federal 36 percent cap on loans to military personnel and their families has stopped the worst payday lender abuses of those serving our country. Our civilian working families are in dire need of the same protections.

Payday lending industry representatives have lobbied for other reforms, such as payment plans and renewal bans, because they understand that these measures have done nothing to slow the rate at which they can flip loans to the same borrowers. But an interest rate cap is the only measure that has proven effective.

Predatory payday lending needs immediate attention, especially in a time where preserving the purchasing power of working families is an essential part of economic recovery.

> *"Payday lenders target military bases all over the country, eager to access a customer base that's often young, financially inexperienced, and especially attractive because of their steady paycheck."*

Payday Lenders Target the Military

Mike Woelflein

Mike Woelflein is a writer who focuses on financial issues concerning veterans. In the following viewpoint, he discusses the disproportionate number of payday lending businesses surrounding military bases. Such businesses target lower-level military personnel because these individuals tend to have low but regular incomes, and are often financially inexperienced and easy to track down. While the military has made efforts to educate troops about the risks of using payday lenders and offers alternative lending options, payday lenders remain attractive to military personnel because they provide instant cash with very few requirements.

As you read, consider the following questions:

1. How do the military's codes of conduct contribute to making troops more susceptible to payday lending, according to the author?

2. How do payday lenders get around state laws prohibiting payday lending, in Mike Woelflein's view?

3. As the author asserts, what does the Pentagon Federal Credit Union require of borrowers to qualify for a loan?

A sailor based at Naval Station Mayport, Florida, needed $300 for car repairs, and needed it fast. He did what a lot of servicemen and women do: He went to one of the "payday" lenders that crowd Mayport Road, and authorized the lender to electronically withdraw $350 from his account on his next payday. The sailor got out of his little car jam, but got himself into a much bigger one.

"When payday comes," said Captain Bill Kennedy, USN [United States Navy] (Ret.), director of the Navy-Marine Corps Relief Society (NMCRS) at Mayport, "he's a little short. He had $347 in his account. Before his check got into his account on that payday, the lending institution hit his account 10 times, and each time the bank charged him a $20 fee for insufficient funds. So when his pay did come, it was about $660. Two hundred went to the bank; $350 went to the lender. And he had about $110 left for two weeks."

Kennedy sees one or two sailors with similar problems every week. Many times, the sailors take one loan, find themselves unable to pay, and roll it over to another loan, doubling the fee. Or, they pay it off with a loan from another lender, and end up starting a vicious spiral of loan-upon-loan that is impossible to escape, with annual interest rates as high as 500 percent.

A Huge Problem

It's not just Mayport, or the Navy. Payday lenders target military bases all over the country, eager to access a customer base that's often young, financially inexperienced, and especially attractive because of their steady paycheck. Signs for "Fast Cash Loans" and "Advance 'Til Payday" are a common sight near military bases. Although some states—among them Georgia—have enacted new laws to try to protect military personnel, the problem continues.

And the problem appears to be growing. In 2002, the NMCRS issued $276,000 interest-free loans to 759 service members. That grew to $514,000 to 1,280 people in 2003, and preliminary numbers show it jumped to between $900,000 and $1 million in 2004.

"It's a huge problem, and we only see the tip of the iceberg," says Admiral Steve Abbot, USN (Ret.), president of NMCRS. "We do provide assistance, but we do so carefully, with the involvement of the command to which they're attached. We also work to bring pressure on payday lenders to reform their practices."

Payday loans, also known as cash advances or deferred deposit loans, offer cash in exchange for a post-dated check or debt authorization. Typically, borrowers put up $350 to get $300, with the loan due in two weeks. If the borrower cannot pay it off after two weeks, there is another $50 charge to extend the loan. These extensions can pile up over months, and force some borrowers to take out more loans from other payday lenders, a cycle that can snowball. Recent news reports tell of a soldier who spent $7,000 to pay off a $1,900 loan, without touching the principal; another borrowed $1,500 and paid $3,000 to clear it.

Targeting the Troops

Payday lenders' best customers are those with low incomes, people who need a $200 to $500 loan for an emergency or a splurge. Lower-level troops fit that category, and offer things most low-income people don't: They are easy to track, they have a steady, government paycheck that is always on schedule. Plus, the military's codes of conduct—and the fear of retribution, even court-martial, for piling up debt—make them susceptible. Many military personnel have a perception that financial trouble could mean career trouble, a part of the culture that inadvertently may help lenders near bases.

"These businesses are right outside the main gate," says Mayport's Kennedy. "They know when the service members get paid, and they're easy prey. These people are 19 to 21 years old, it's their first time on their own, their first time managing their money, and they have very little spare money. So if they goof, that's where they go."

The payday lending industry claims it does not target the military. But a forthcoming study by University of Florida assistant professor Christopher Peterson and California State-Northridge professor Steven Graves, will clearly show that they do.

Graves and Peterson looked at 20 of the largest military bases in the country, comparing the density of payday lenders to the number of banks near bases, and the base area's zip code to other areas of the state. Marines from Camp Pendleton, California, do a lot of their off-base business in Oceanside, California. Within three miles of the base there are 24 payday lenders—22 in Oceanside—compared to 26 banks. Nearby Carlsbad, which is demographically similar but farther from the base, has eight payday lenders and 29 banks.

"The number one zip code for payday lenders in more than a handful of states is directly adjacent to a military base," Graves says. "It's the same thing all over. The data say, are these people attracted to areas of poverty? Yes, sort of. Are they attracted to minorities? Yes, sort of. The military? Yes, definitely."

What's Being Done?

Troop education is one key to avoiding the payday loans. All of the services offer financial training to their members. At Naval Submarine Base Kings Bay in Georgia, the Fleet and Family Support Center provides budgeting classes and services, debt management programs, as well as training on car and home buying, investments, and other topics. They try to steer sailors to the Navy Federal Credit Union and, if they are financially troubled, to the NMCRS.

"We try to get them to see how it snowballs," says Felipe Gonzalez, a civilian financial counselor at the Fleet and Family Support Center, Naval Submarine Base Kings Bay. "We have sample contracts where we black out the person's name and show them how high the interest rate is, and how they get away with charging 360 percent. They just don't realize."

But clearly, education isn't enough. Steve Tripoli, a consumer advocate at the National Consumer Law Center (NCLC) and the primary author of the nonprofit group's *In Harm's Way—At Home* study of consumer scams and their effects on the military, believes that educational efforts could be both expanded and improved.

In some states, legislation has helped mitigate the issue. In April 2004, Georgia enacted a law that was intended to rid the state of predatory lenders by making the practice akin to racketeering.

"It has gotten better," says Gonzalez, the financial counselor. "We had five or six of these places here, and we're down to one."

Still, payday lending remains legal in 36 states. Plus, lenders have found ways to get around the laws in numerous ways. Some set up across state lines, or funnel loans through out-of-state banks. Still more have turned to the Internet, which allows them to base their operations in areas—even offshore—

Where Payday Lenders Are Concentrated

Nearly every statistical measure we used at every spatial scale points to the same conclusion: The payday loan industry targets military personnel. The evidence is overwhelming and incontrovertible. Our overall analysis included 20 states; 1,516 counties; 13,253 zip codes; and nearly 15,000 payday lenders. Situated among those many counties and zip codes were 109 military bases and several dozen recently closed bases. Within three miles of open bases were 150 counties and 813 zip codes. Payday lenders were in these military-adjacent counties and zip codes at greater numbers and in greater densities in almost every state we examined. These counties and zip codes represent a wide range of ethnic, income, and population characteristics and none of these variables account for the clarity of pattern that we have witnessed. With striking regularity, the counties and zip codes most overrepresented by payday lenders had one thing in common: large military populations.

Steven M. Graves and Christopher L. Peterson,
"Predatory Lending and the Military:
The Law and Geography of 'Payday' Loans in Military Towns,"
Ohio State Law Journal, vol. 66, no. 4, 2005.

where such loans are legal. Others market themselves as catalog sales companies, disguising fees as payment for merchandise coupons.

Payday Lenders Versus Credit Unions and Navy-Marine Corps Relief Society

Why do service members go to these lenders rather than borrow from the NMCRS or a base credit union? For the most part, the interest-free loans or grants from NMCRS are only for service members in true financial crises. For the most part, those who access payday lenders are financially unsophisticated borrowers looking for a quick loan to tide them over to payday. The payday lenders are easier and faster to deal with— and take full advantage of the situation.

A typical short-term loan from a credit union or bank more than likely has an interest rate of 18 percent or less, and often allows a borrower who is unable to pay it back on time to roll the loan over without additional fees. But they also might take several days to process; by the time a service member walks into a payday lender, his or her problem could require instant access to cash. Finally, borrowing from a bank or credit union may be difficult for those with bad credit histories, whereas a payday lender requires little more than proof of employment.

Some credit unions, such as Pentagon Federal Credit Union (PFCU), have started new programs that offer emergency cash in 30 minutes or less, often through nonprofit subsidiaries. At PFCU, borrowers pay a flat fee of $6 for any loan amount up to a maximum of $500, considerably less than most payday lenders charge. These programs often have limits, such as no more than five loans or rollovers in a 12-month period, and many including PFCU require borrowers to attend financial counseling sessions in order to qualify.

Using the Political Power of the Military

What can military leaders do to combat this problem? Experts inside and outside the armed forces say it's important for leaders to speak out to legislative leaders, both locally and nationally. Those voices are all the louder in states where bases are economically important.

"The best way that the military could go about solving this problem is to use its political leadership and leverage," says Peterson, the study's author. "If they want to protect the troops, they should support interest-rate caps, and they should not underestimate the power of their voice. They have enormous credibility and when they say, 'Our soldiers need to be protected,' there are a lot of people who will listen."

High-ranking Defense Department officials are using their clout. In Georgia and in other states, military leaders have pressured state officials to deal with the issue of payday lending with some serious political clout: the omnipresent threat of base closure. No local or state politician wants to be viewed as the one who let a base close. With a round of closures coming down the pike, DoD [Department of Defense] has let legislators know that a failure to address predatory lending practices near military bases could be seen as a negative when evaluating a facility.

Recent anti-predatory loan laws in Georgia, Illinois, Virginia and Florida all came about in part because of the efforts of military leaders who have spoken out or testified before legislative bodies.

"I don't believe this is simply a state issue," says NMCRS's Admiral Abbot. "Banking is generally a state regulation operation, but I think because of the victimization of servicemen and women, it becomes a federal issue and one that Congress should undertake and control."

Limiting Loans and Lenders

There is hope. Representative Sam Graves (R-Mo.) sponsored a bill late in November 2004, to cap interest rates at 36 percent annually. According to a Graves spokesman, the service members Anti-Predatory Lending Protection Act would also limit the number of rollover loans permitted. The bill didn't get anywhere last year [2004], in part because it was introduced so late. But Graves reintroduced H.R. 97 early this year [2005], with plenty of time for it to gather the legislature's attention. As of late January [2005], the bill was in the hands of the House Committee on Veterans' Affairs. As Representative

Graves noted: "These businesses are geared toward and targeting our soldiers. Our men and women in uniform should not be treated like a niche market; we depend on them for our freedom and owe them our gratitude."

Beyond legislation, there are other ways of controlling payday lenders. The NCLC's Tripoli says military police and Judge Advocate General's Corps should crack down on the places that are violating laws. He also suggests creating partnerships with state attorney general offices, local law enforcement, private lawyers willing to fight predatory lending and even the Federal Trade Commission. Several experts, including Tripoli, believe base commanders should make payday lenders off-limits to personnel.

"When it does happen, these lenders either shut down or they end up negotiating with the base leaders, and that can help get their interest rates under control," Tripoli says.

Another suggestion from Tripoli is to limit advertisement in base newspapers and even the Army/Navy/Air Force/Marine Corps *Times* newspapers, which are published by Gannett.

Troops Need More Help

Finally, experts say that commanding officers should give their charges a better idea of where they can seek help if they do have financial problems. Better interest rates are available at banks and base credit unions.

In the Navy, every unit has a required number of command financial specialists, first-class or above, service members who have been trained to help colleagues to plan budgets, deal with bad credit, and assist family members.

"I'd like to see division officers and commanding officers talk to their men and women more about this," Kennedy says. "If you are having a problem, we have expert people on board who can help. I wish every serviceman and woman could be warned, 'Don't go to these payday lenders.'"

> "[Payday] lenders are increasingly targeting recipients of Social Security and other government benefits, including disability and veteran's benefits."

Payday Lenders Target the Elderly and Disabled

Ellen E. Schultz and Theo Francis

Ellen E. Schultz and Theo Francis write about finance for the Wall Street Journal. In this viewpoint, they assert that the payday lending industry is pursuing customers who receive regular government checks, such as the elderly and disabled, more than ever before. Studies show that payday lenders are often disproportionately located near government-subsidized housing for these populations. Not only are such customers attractive because of their stable incomes, but they are also frequently unable to pay off loans. Because they do not have the option of working to settle their loans, they often become trapped in debt.

As you read, consider the following questions:

1. What legal change do the authors cite from the late 1990s that made it easier for Social Security recipients to get payday loans?

2. In what way do Social Security recipients supposedly enjoy more legal protections than other borrowers, according to federal law?

3. How do many payday lenders manage to seize borrowers' government benefits in spite of the law, according to the authors?

One recent morning, dozens of elderly and disabled people, some propped on walkers and canes, gathered at Small Loans Inc. Many had borrowed money from Small Loans and turned over their Social Security benefits to pay back the high-interest lender. Now they were waiting for their "allowance"—their monthly check, minus Small Loans' cut.

The crowd represents the newest twist for a fast-growing industry—lenders that make high-interest loans, often called "payday" loans, that are secured by upcoming paychecks. Such lenders are increasingly targeting recipients of Social Security and other government benefits, including disability and veteran's benefits. "These people always get paid, rain or shine," says William Harrod, a former manager of payday loan stores in suburban Virginia and Washington, D.C. Government beneficiaries "will always have money, every 30 days."

The law bars the government from sending a recipient's benefits directly to lenders. But many of these lenders are forging relationships with banks and arranging for prospective borrowers to have their benefits checks deposited directly into bank accounts. The banks immediately transfer government funds to the lenders. The lender then subtracts debt repayments, plus fees and interest, before giving the recipients a dime.

As a result, these lenders, which pitch loans with effective annual interest as high as 400% or more, can gain almost total control over Social Security recipients' finances.

There are no publicly available statistics on the proportion of payday loans that are backed by Social Security and other government benefits. But dozens of legal aid lawyers, senior service groups, and credit counselors across the country say they are seeing more and more clients on Social Security struggling with multiple payday loans.

A Captive Market

The Treasury Department, charged with ensuring that Social Security payments reach beneficiaries, says privacy rules forbid it from monitoring recipients' bank accounts without cause. Social Security Administration officials say the agency isn't responsible for benefits once paid out and that beneficiaries who run into problems should consult an attorney.

An analysis of data from the U.S. Department of Housing and Urban Development shows many payday lenders are clustered around government-subsidized housing for seniors and the disabled. The research was done by Steven Graves, a geographer at California State University at Northridge, at the *Wall Street Journal's* request. His previous work was cited by the Department of Defense in its effort to cap the amounts lenders can charge military personnel.

Lenders say they provide a useful service. "This industry provides convenient access to small amounts of money," said Tommy Moore, executive vice president of the Community Financial Services Association of America, which says it represents about 60% of payday loan stores. "It certainly wouldn't be right for the business to discriminate against them for whatever the source of their income is."

But some industry critics say fixed-income borrowers are not only more reliable, they are also more lucrative. Often elderly or disabled, they are typically dependent on smaller fixed incomes and are rarely able to pay off their loans quickly. "It's not like they can work more hours," says David Rothstein, an analyst at Policy Matters Ohio, an economic research group in Cleveland. "They're trapped."

Targeting a Vulnerable Group

Mr. Harrod was a manager of a Check 'n Go store across the street from Fort Lincoln Senior Citizens Village, a subsidized-housing complex for the elderly and disabled in Washington, D.C. Mr. Harrod says he was encouraged by his supervisors to recruit the elderly, and did so by often eating his lunch on nearby benches to strike up conversations with the complex's residents. According to Mr. Graves's analysis, there are at least four payday lenders within a mile-and-a-half of Fort Lincoln.

Mr. Harrod quit his job in August [2007] over concerns that the company exploited its customers and targeted vulnerable groups and began working with groups seeking limits on payday lending.

Yancy Deering, a spokesman for Check 'n Go [CNG], a unit of closely held Ohio-based CNG Holdings, Inc., which has more than 1,300 stores nationwide, confirms Mr. Harrod's tenure but says the company doesn't target the elderly. He adds the company doesn't track what proportion of customers depend on government benefits.

Social Security recipients weren't always a natural market for payday lenders, which typically require borrowers to have a bank account and a regular source of income. For years, a large percentage of government beneficiaries lacked traditional bank accounts, choosing to just cash their checks instead.

But by the late 1990s, the federal government began requiring that Social Security beneficiaries receive their benefits by electronic deposit to a bank account, unless they opt out. The number of recipients with direct deposit soared to more than 80% today, up from 56% in 1996. Citing taxpayer savings and greater security and convenience for recipients, the government is making a fresh push to get the remaining hold-outs to participate.

A Booming Industry

With direct deposit, Social Security recipients could now more easily pledge their future checks as collateral for small short-term loans. Oliver Hummel, a Billings, Montana, resident with schizophrenia, lived on the $1,013 a month in Social Security disability benefits he received by direct deposit to his bank account. Early last year [2007], after his car broke down and his 13-year-old terrier racked up a big vet bill, Mr. Hummel borrowed $200 from a local lender.

Like many payday borrowers, Mr. Hummel realized he couldn't pay off the loan when it was due so he went to another "payday" lender. Lenders rarely ask about other loans and debt, and borrowers often take out multiple loans in an effort to avoid defaulting. By February [2007], Mr. Hummel had eight loans from eight lenders, at effective annual interest rates that ranged from 180% to 406%.

The industry mushroomed in the 1990s and continues to prosper. Analysts estimate that payday loan volume has climbed to about $48 billion a year from about $13.8 billion in 1999. Most payday lenders are small and privately held. The biggest publicly traded company is Advance America Cash Advance Centers Inc., based in Spartanburg, South Carolina, with 2,900 stores in three dozen states and reported earnings of $42.9 million in the first nine months of 2007.

An Inadequate Allowance

In November 2002, when Melvin Bevels was short of money for groceries and rent, the elderly man visited a Small Loans store in Sylacauga, Alabama, and borrowed money—he thinks it was $200. Small Loans is part of a sprawling network of more than a hundred lenders in four states, including Georgia, Florida, and Louisiana, owned by Money Tree Inc., a closely held Bainbridge, Georgia, firm.

Mr. Bevels, who can't read, says a clerk helped him fill out papers that instructed Social Security to send Mr. Bevels's $565 monthly benefits to an account at an out-of-state bank, which transferred the money back to Small Loans or its parent, usually within a day. As is often the case, Mr. Bevels's bank earned no interest and didn't come with either ATM cards or checks.

Every month for nearly four years, Mr. Bevels, who is known around town as "Buckwheat" because of his thatch of yellow-white hair, rode his motorized mobility scooter to Small Loans to pick up his "allowance," which was sometimes as little as $180 a month, he says.

In a written statement, Money Tree's general counsel, Natasha Wood, declined to comment on Mr. Bevels's case but said: "Anyone who sets up a direct deposit arrangement with Small Loans Inc. does so completely voluntarily."

Mr. Bevels, who believes he's 80 but isn't sure, quickly lost control of his finances. When his utilities were shut off, a neighbor gave Mr. Bevels water in a plastic jug and ran an extension cord to Mr. Bevels's trailer a few hours a day to power his nebulizer, which delivers aerosol medication to people with chronic lung conditions. Mr. Bevels was facing eviction when his trailer burned down, leaving him homeless.

Borrowers Can Lose More than Benefits

A county social worker arranged for Mr. Bevels to move to public housing and got his Social Security benefits redirected to a local bank. When Small Loans sued Mr. Bevels for repayment in small-claims court in Talladega County, Alabama, a legal aid attorney headed to court. The judge threw out the case when the lender failed to appear with documentation for the loan.

"It just isn't fair, what they do to old people," says Mr. Bevels, crying quietly. "It isn't right."

Ms. Wood, the lawyer for Small Loans, said in her statement: "Small Loans Inc. does not file suit against anyone because they move their direct deposit service elsewhere."

No regulatory agency tracks how much Social Security money is going to lenders as repayment for payday loans. A 2006 study by the Consumer Federation of America found that one-fifth of those without conventional bank accounts are receiving their government benefit checks through non-banks, including payday lenders that also operate as check-cashing stores.

Social Security recipients are supposed to enjoy more protections than other borrowers: Federal law says that creditors can't seize Social Security benefits to repay debts. Small Loans and two banks with which it has partnered say their arrangements don't violate any laws. But critics say such arrangements effectively thwart the intention of the law. Social Security recipients can not only lose their benefits, but face lawsuits, harassment and even jail.

Interest and Fees Leave Customers Little to Live On

In December 2006, Jennifer Rumph, a disabled single mother of three, went to Miracle Finance Inc. to buy her children a computer for Christmas. She picked a laptop from the store's catalog and the Miracle Finance clerk said it would cost a little over $600, Ms. Rumph recalls. Some lenders have catalogs of merchandise and lend money to make the purchase. In the end, the loan came to $1,326, which included principal, interest and a fee for insurance that would pay off the loan to the lender if Ms. Rumph died, according to loan paperwork.

The company had Ms. Rumph, 43, sign documents directing her teenage son's Social Security disability check, which is $623 a month, to the company by way of an intermediary

Payday Lenders Go After Social Security Recipients

Payday lenders have been accused of targeting Social Security beneficiaries, whose monthly checks from Uncle Sam make them especially attractive...

Law prohibits the government from sending Social Security checks directly to lenders. But by establishing relationships with banks, lenders can pressure borrowers to have their Social Security checks deposited directly into those third-party accounts, say consumer advocates.

Sid Kirchheimer, "Payday Lenders Target Social Security Recipients," AARP Bulletin Today, June 6, 2008.

bank—a condition for getting the loan, she says. The Social Security Administration says it doesn't have a problem with lenders capturing Social Security checks of disabled or orphaned children as long as the benefits money ultimately goes to the "current needs" of the child.

Like Mr. Bevels, Ms. Rumph didn't receive an ATM card or a checkbook. Each month she would go to Miracle Finance 30 miles away in Abbeville, Alabama, to pick up what remained of her son Jeremiah's benefits after the company subtracted fees, interest and loan repayments, usually leaving her with less than $300 of her son's check.

Ms. Rumph, whose medical problems include severe asthma and two hip replacements, was unable to pay her bills on that amount. Much of the $623-a-month in disability benefits she receives for herself was going to a nearby Small Loans store to repay a different loan. She tried to return the computer, but a Miracle Finance employee said it wouldn't reduce her debt, and then the computer stopped working this summer, she recalls.

Some Recipients Are Unaware of Their Rights

In the following months, Ms. Rumph says she asked Social Security several times to redirect her son's check to her mailbox, but to little avail.

Attorneys for Legal Services Alabama, whom Ms. Rumph ultimately contacted, say that each time she tried to cancel the arrangement, the company appears to have resubmitted her original direct-deposit paperwork, which Social Security honored despite her efforts to cancel it.

A Social Security spokeswoman says that when beneficiaries cancel direct-deposit arrangements with the agency, they should also contact the bank that had been receiving the check. Ms. Rumph says she never knew the identity of the bank receiving her son's Social Security benefits.

After Ms. Rumph fell behind on her payments, Miracle Finance sued her in small-claims court in Abbeville, Alabama. Although federal law says creditors can't seize Social Security, disability, and veteran's benefits to pay a debt, enforcement of the law is scant, and many Social Security recipients are unaware of their legal rights. Lenders and their debt collectors routinely sue Social Security recipients who fall behind in their payments, and threaten them with criminal prosecution, senior advocates say.

Debtors must go to court to prove their case. Ms. Rumph says she didn't know any of this and was afraid to go to court. Miracle Finance won a $1,500 default judgment in July [2007], and four days later sought a court order requiring Ms. Rumph to appear in person to detail her income and assets.

After Ms. Rumph failed to appear at two hearings at Miracle Finance's request, a judge ordered a warrant for her arrest.

Debt Still Looms

In November [2007], Miracle Finance kept the full amount of Jeremiah Rumph's disability check. Ms. Rumph fell behind on her $300-a-month rent for her mobile home and faced eviction. After she was unable to pay utility bills, her electricity was turned off briefly the day before Thanksgiving.

On Sunday, Dec. 9 [2007], as she was getting ready for church, two sheriff's deputies came to Ms. Rumph's home, handcuffed her in front of her children and hauled her away. Ms. Rumph spent several hours in jail until an uncle paid the court $1,500. Miracle Finance didn't respond to numerous requests for comment.

A judge last week [February, 2008] said Miracle Finance couldn't force Ms. Rumph to pay the debt because her Social Security income is protected under federal law. But she still owes more than $5,000 on loans from almost a dozen other lenders. "I want to pay them back," she says. "I can't."

> "States should act to implement legislation preventing predatory payday lending practices."

The Government Should Protect Citizens from Predatory Payday Lenders

Alexander Bartik et al.

The authors of the following viewpoint argue that payday lending undermines the economic security of working individuals and families. The authors contend that the exorbitant fees and annual percentage rates charged by payday lenders trap consumers in an endless cycle of debt. It is the government that allows these lenders to charge such exorbitant rates, they argue, and it is the government that must protect society's most vulnerable citizens from these predatory lending practices. They believe that by structuring laws to close readily exploited loopholes, states can effectively prevent the predatory payday lending practices that exploit the desperation of America's workers.

Alexander Bartik et al., "Predatory Payday Lending Reform," *Policy Studies Journal*, vol. 35, no. 3, 2007, pp. 516–517. Copyright © 2007 Policy Studies Organization. Reproduced by permission.

As you read, consider the following questions:

1. According to the viewpoint, how much does the typical borrower end up paying in order to fully pay off a loan of $325?

2. What is the Talent-Nelson Amendment?

3. What are some alternatives to payday loans mentioned in the viewpoint?

Payday lending undermines the economic security of working individuals and families. Many low-income workers, lacking the credit history and collateral needed to obtain a traditional loan but still in need of quick cash, turn to payday lenders who require only a bank account.

The borrower gives a postdated personal check to the lender in return for cash. In most cases, however, borrowers are unable to fully repay their debt, and they consequently, incur repeated bounced check fees. The rolled-over long-term loans have annual percentage rates (APRs) of interest ranging from 391 to 443 percent on average. These exorbitant fees and APRs trap needy consumers in endless cycles of debt. Because borrowers are unable to pay off an initial loan, 91 percent of all loans go to borrowers with at least 5 payday loans per year. As a result, the typical borrower ends up paying a total of $793 in order to fully pay off a loan of $325.

History of the Payday Loan Industry

The predatory payday loan industry has undergone a massive expansion over the past few years. A $10 billion national industry in 2000, payday lending grew to a $28 billion industry by 2006. In 2006, the 109th Congress recognized the serious threat predatory payday lending practices pose to the economic security of working Americans, passing the Talent-Nelson Amendment to cap APR rates on all short-term loans to military personnel at 36 percent.

Many states have attempted to regulate lending practices, though to date, only a handful have managed to close the loopholes readily exploited by predatory lenders.

By comparing the laws of states that have successfully prohibited predatory payday lending with those that have not, we can understand how to close loopholes and prohibit these exploitative practices across the country. Illinois legislation passed in 2001 and 2005 has overwhelmingly failed to prevent predatory practices because the laws target specific loan lengths. For example, when lenders were prohibited from charging high interest rates on loans shorter than 30 days, they immediately began offering 31-day loans with the same high APRs.

Connecticut, on the other hand, uses a broad usury law, capping all small loan APRs at a more reasonable rate. This has effectively prevented predatory payday lending in the state. Around the country, the market for predatory payday loans is driven by a lack of knowledge about alternatives and consequences, so credit counseling and education services should accompany any usury regulations.

Payday Lending Regulation

Predatory payday lending regulation can be implemented on the state or national level. Each state has its own banking and usury laws, and successful regulation generally expands these laws to better regulate payday lenders. National legislation would also be effective. Education and credit counseling services can be developed on any level, though the responsibility for implementation will ultimately rest with local communities.

States should act to implement legislation preventing predatory payday lending practices. Laws must be broad, placing APR caps on all small loans, and applying to all citizens. This way, lenders will be unable to continue modifying loan terms to avoid regulation. State regulations on short-term

Some State Governments Have Banned or Limited Payday Lending

After three years of grassroots efforts and several failed attempts to pass statewide legislation to abolish payday lending, in March [2008] the Virginia legislature approved the first piece of legislation to regulate the industry. . . .

Similar fights have also been waged or are underway at the state level in many of the other 37 states that allow payday lending. The North Carolina legislature successfully booted lenders from the state in 2001 by allowing the sunset provision that the industry was operating under expire. In Arkansas, though the state constitution prohibits lenders from charging more than 17 percent interest, payday lenders have been allowed to operate there for years. But in mid-March [2008], the state attorney general sent a letter to all the payday lenders in the state, telling them to shut down operations immediately and void customers' debts. Several other states have capped interest rates at 36 percent, and last September [2007], Washington, D.C., passed a law capping the rate at 24 percent. A number of other states are also currently considering bills to regulate the industry.

Kate Sheppard, "An End to Payday Loans?"
American Prospect, *May 6, 2008.*

loans should include several stipulations. A "cooling-off period," when borrowers are limited to one loan at a time and must wait 15 days between paying off one loan and taking out another, along with a cap limiting loan rollovers to two, will help prevent consumers from getting trapped in an endless cycle of debt.

Alternatives to payday loans do exist, and borrowers should be informed of these alternatives. Credit unions, social service programs, charities and faith-based organizations throughout the country offer assistance to individuals in financial need, both in the form of loans and free credit counseling. All states also have winter heating cost assistance programs aimed at eliminating a major cause of payday loan demand. Public education campaigns should be established to inform individuals that payday loans are not the only option for fast cash.

| *"You can't make people better off by taking options away from them."*

The Government Should Allow Citizens the Choice to Use Payday Lenders

George Leef

In this viewpoint, George Leef discusses North Carolina's 2006 law banning payday lending. He argues that such a move does not make poor people better off; instead, it takes away options from them. Leef questions the logic of the assertion made by defenders of the law that payday lenders aren't missed in North Carolina. In fact, he says, payday lenders are most certainly missed by their former customers, who are now forced to use less attractive loan options. Leef is vice president for research at the John William Pope Center for Higher Education Policy in North Carolina.

As you read, consider the following questions:

1. In the telephone survey conducted by the UNC (University of North Carolina) Center for Community Capital, what ratio of respondents said payday lending was a "bad thing"?

George Leef, "Banning Payday Loans Deprives Low-Income People of Options," *Freeman: Ideas on Liberty*, vol. 58, April 2008, pp. 17–18. Copyright © 2008 Foundation for Economic Education, Incorporated. www.fee.org. All rights reserved. Reproduced by permission. www.thefreemanonline.org.

2. What does George Leef feel would have been a more accurate summary of how North Carolina's residents feel about the ban on payday lending?

3. According to Thomas Lehman, what is the effect of preventing or limiting the use of payday loans on borrowers?

In 2006 North Carolina joined a growing list of states that ban "payday lending." Payday loans are small, short-term loans made to workers to provide them with cash until their next paychecks. This kind of borrowing is costly, reflecting both the substantial risk of nonpayment and high overhead costs of dealing with many little transactions. I wouldn't borrow money that way, but there is enough demand for such loans to support thousands of payday-lending stores across the nation. They make several million loans each year.

But no longer in North Carolina.

Pointing to the high cost of payday borrowing, a coalition of groups claiming to represent the poor stampeded the North Carolina General Assembly into putting all the payday lenders out of business. The reason I'm writing about this now is that the North Carolina Office of the Commissioner of Banks recently felt the need to justify the ban with the release of a study purporting to demonstrate that the politicians did the right thing. How do they know? Because payday lending "is not missed." The preposterous lack of logic in this whole exercise cannot pass without comment.

Before we look at the defense that has been given for this nanny state dictate, we should consider what I call Sowell's Axiom: You can't make people better off by taking options away from them. (It's named for the economist Thomas Sowell, one of whose books drove this point home to me many years ago.)

An individual will act to further his self-interest, and in doing so, will choose the course of action that is most likely to succeed. Sometimes a person faces difficult circumstances and has to choose the option that's least bad. But that doesn't change the analysis. If he's out of money and needs cash until his next paycheck, he will have to consider various unpleasant alternatives and choose the best one.

The Least Bad Option

Obtaining money through a payday loan works like this: The borrower, after proving to the lender that he is employed and has sufficient income, writes a check to the lender postdated to his next payday for some amount, say, $300. The lender gives him a smaller amount of cash, say, $260. The lender then cashes the check on its due date. That is obviously a very high annual rate of interest if you consider the $40 fee as an interest charge. A payday loan is not an attractive option—unless all your others are worse. No one would do it unless every other course of action looked even costlier.

Nevertheless, the North Carolinians who worked to abolish payday lending are eager to say they did no harm. A group called the UNC [University of North Carolina] Center for Community Capital conducted a telephone survey of 400 low- and middle-income families in the state about how they deal with financial shortfalls. Only 159 reported having had financial troubles they couldn't meet out of their regular income. From this small number of responses, the people doing the study concluded that "Payday lending is not missed." That's because, based on the telephone surveys, "almost nine out of ten said payday lending was a 'bad thing' and 'twice as many respondents said the absence of payday lending has had a positive effect on their household than said it has had a negative effect.'"

There you have it. Most people said payday lending was "bad" and few miss it now that it has been banned. That certainly proves that the state did the right thing in getting rid of it. Or does it?

An Option Taken Away

Completely forgotten in the rush to justify the ban are the people who said they think they *are* worse off for not having this option anymore. Yes, they were a minority of the respondents, but that is no reason to conclude that "payday lending is not missed." An accurate conclusion would instead be, "Payday lending is missed by some people."

Maybe the silliness of this approach will be apparent if we consider a hypothetical case that parallels it.

Imagine that a group of people in New York hates opera. They regard it as too costly and time-consuming, and a bad moral influence. Using their political connections, they succeed in getting the city government to ban live opera productions. Out goes the Met, the Civic Opera, and any other companies.

A year later this group commissions a survey asking 400 New Yorkers if they miss having opera in the city. Since most people don't care about or even dislike opera, the results come in showing that the overwhelming majority of New Yorkers agree "Opera is not missed." Would that justify taking opera away from the, say, 5 percent who said they would like to have had the option of going?

My point is that the views of the people who don't patronize a business or art form shouldn't count for anything. The people who don't like opera are free not to go, and the people who think payday lending is "bad" are free to avoid it. As long as anyone wants to attend an opera or needs a payday loan, the government has no business forcibly depriving them of those choices.

Better than the Alternatives

Returning to the North Carolina study, people were also asked how they respond when they have a money shortage. The results showed that people coped in various ways, including

Bans on Payday Lending Are Paternalistic

The message sent by lawmakers who want to ban payday lending is to declare that consumers capable of opening a checking account and earning a paycheck can't act like adults when it comes to managing a three-figure loan. This lesson from government will only erode personal responsibility to the detriment of a healthy society.

Americans don't need their money managed by paternalist politicians.

Tim Miller, "Ban Payday Loans? Big Mistake,"
Christian Science Monitor, *May 6, 2008.*

paying bills late, dipping into savings, borrowing from family or friends, using a credit card to get cash, or merely doing without things. Jumping on that information, North Carolina's deputy commissioner of banks, Mark Pearce, said in the November 14, 2007, Raleigh *News & Observer,* "Working people don't miss payday lending. They have a lot of financial options and they use them."

We can only wonder why it doesn't occur to Pearce that having *one more* option might be good. What if someone has already exhausted all possible money sources and faces serious consequences from either paying late (suppose the next missed payment means the power gets turned off) or doing without (you've got to have some car repairs so you can get to work)? A payday loan might be the best option left.

In an August 2006 paper on the payday lending business (*Payday Lending and Public Policy: What Elected Officials Should Know*), Professor Thomas Lehman of Indiana Wesleyan University found that this kind of lending fills a market niche and concluded, "Preventing or limiting the use of payday loan services only encourages borrowers to seek out and utilize less attractive alternatives ... that put the borrower in an even weaker financial position."

A November 2007 study by two economists with the Federal Reserve Bank of New York (*Payday Holiday: How Households Fare After Payday Credit Bans*) came to the same conclusion. Authors Donald Morgan and Michael Strain found that a ban on payday lending results in increased credit problems for consumers. They wrote, "Payday credit is preferable to substitutes such as the bounced-check 'protection' sold by credit unions and banks or loans from pawnshops."

So I maintain that Sowell's Axiom holds. When government takes away options, it is bound to make some people worse off. Instead of acting like Big Nanny, government should stick to enforcing laws against coercion and fraud.

Periodical Bibliography

The following articles have been selected to supplement the diverse views presented in this chapter.

Angela Couloumbis   "Two Moves to Control Payday Lending," *Philadelphia Inquirer*, December 6, 2005.

Robert DeYoung   "Congress Takes Aim at Payday Loans," *Wall Street Journal*, April 14, 2009.

Marc Fisher   "Are Payday Loans a Service or a Disservice?" *Washington Post*, January 20, 2008.

Robert H. Frank   "Payday Loans Are a Scourge, but Should Wrath Be Aimed at the Lenders?" *New York Times*, January 18, 2007.

Sue Kirchhoff   "Breaking the Cycle of Payday Loan 'Trap,'" *USA Today*, September 20, 2006.

Ed Lazere   "Good Riddance to Payday Lending in DC," *Capital Community News*, September 2007.

Douglas McGray   "Check Cashers, Redeemed," *New York Times Magazine*, November 9, 2008.

Joyce Moed   "Alternative Payday Loan Program Benefits Members, Their CU," *Credit Union Journal*, December 22, 2008.

Alec Schierenbeck   "No Credit? No Collateral? No Problem," *Iowa Independent*, August 6, 2008.

Michelle Singletary   "Payday Loans: Costly Cash," *Washington Post*, February 25, 2007.

CHAPTER 3

Is Peer-to-Peer Lending an Effective Alternative to Traditional Lending?

Chapter Preface

Online peer-to-peer lending, in which people in need of loans and people with money to loan connect on Web sites such as Prosper and the Lending Club, is a relatively new industry, but many say it is really just a new twist on an old concept. In an *Information Week* article by Thomas Claburn, Prosper CEO and cofounder Chris Larsen said that online lending "goes back to the way things used to be . . . when one neighbor supported the business of another neighbor." Larsen believes this community lending model is a good one because "there was a really strong sense of obligation and accountability and reputation within a small community, which actually made repayment of debts more reliable and less risky." Indeed, Prosper's own Web site explains that the roots of peer lending "date back well into the most ancient of all civilizations," including Mesopotamia, Babylon, and ancient Greece.

Lending among community members isn't only an ancient practice; it's still practiced in many cultures, particularly in the developing world. A 2006 *BusinessWeek* article told the story of the Lam family, who fled Vietnam in 1983, and moved to San Jose, California. Supporting seven people in a studio apartment, "the Lams tapped into their local *hoi*, a cooperative of Vietnamese neighbors who pooled money to lend one another."

With the advent of the Internet, though, the opportunities offered by peer-to-peer lending have exploded, because the numbers of borrowers and lenders have increased exponentially. One's community of available borrowers and lenders is no longer confined by geography; a person with money in France can lend to a person in need of money in Thailand. As Hiawatha Bray wrote in the *Boston Globe*, "So-called 'peer-to-peer lending' is another example of how the Internet reshapes nearly every industry it touches."

One difference between online peer lending and traditional peer lending is the presence of an overseeing company that manages agreements between online lenders and borrowers. Companies such as Prosper have set up a streamlined process to screen potential borrowers and lenders and a set of regulations that aim to protect both. In 2008, the U.S. Securities and Exchange Commission (SEC) began regulating these companies as well—a move that many have protested. Government regulation is one of many issues that surround the advent of online peer-to-peer lending. With this industry continuing to grow at a steady pace—even in the face of government regulation—it is imperative that American consumers be aware of the opportunities presented by this new form of lending and the potential risks posed by it. These issues are explored from several vantage points by the authors in this chapter.

"As the credit crunch makes getting a loan even harder for small business owners, for-profit social lending could play a bigger role in financing small enterprises in the U.S."

Peer-to-Peer Lending Offers Small Business Owners a Beneficial Alternative to Banks

John Tozzi

In the following viewpoint, John Tozzi talks about the opportunity peer-to-peer lending sites offer to small businesses, especially in a tight credit market. These lending sites generally provide better turnaround time and use more flexible criteria for evaluating applicants than banks do. In Tozzi's view, because borrowers on lending sites are exposed to thousands of potential lenders at once, they have a better chance of obtaining a loan than they would with a bank. Tozzi writes about small business for BusinessWeek.

John Tozzi, "Will a Stranger Lend You $25,000?" *BusinessWeek*, December 21, 2007. Copyright © 2007 by The McGraw-Hill Companies, Inc. Reprinted by special permission.

As you read, consider the following questions:

1. According to the article, what percentage of loans on peer lending sites are for businesses?

2. As John Tozzi reports, what strategy do peer lending sites advise lenders to use to reduce financial risk?

3. Why did Prosper understand Chris Lindgren's business better than bank officers did, in Lindgren's estimation?

Chris Lindgren needed money. His textbook price comparison site, Direct Textbook, depends mainly on the referral fees it gets when college kids buy books through it. But this past August, the four-year-old business had already used up most of its cash on online advertising, with weeks of the back-to-school rush season still ahead. Lindgren wanted to buy more ads, but revenue from previous sales wouldn't come in for months. His profitable three-employee company had tapped out two lines of credit worth $60,000 from banks in Salem, Ore., where the business is based, and had been turned down by two more.

The day the last loan officer rejected his application, Lindgren heard about Prosper. The auction-style site connects borrowers with lenders and promises both sides more favorable interest rates than banks by cutting overhead costs. Lindgren applied for the maximum $25,000 loan the next day, offering to pay 17.5% interest. Lenders found the offer so attractive that they bid the rate down to 10.2%, and Direct Textbook had the cash in its account within two weeks. The rate is comparable to what Lindgren pays on his bank credit lines.

"Considering our credit situation, I might have ended up paying more," he says.

An Alternative to Banks

Prosper, based in San Francisco, is one of a tiny but growing number of for-profit online social lending marketplaces in the

U.S., which some entrepreneurs are looking to as alternatives to bank loans. (The original concept of making small loans available to people with no collateral in the developing world started in the 1970s and has been growing steadily more popular, sparking praise, controversy, and nonprofit successes like Kiva.) As the credit crunch makes getting a loan even harder for small business owners, for-profit social lending could play a bigger role in financing small enterprises in the U.S. Most sites reported that between 20% to 30% of loans are for businesses; it is the second most common reason borrowers listed, after refinancing debt.

Three companies besides Prosper offer similar services in the U.S.: Zopa, Lending Club, and Virgin Money. Zopa just began lending in the U.S. on Dec. 4; the site operated in Britain for about two years before that. Lending Club, which started as a Facebook application in May, became available in all 50 states on Dec 13. Virgin Money, originally CircleLending, doesn't connect lenders and borrowers, but it formalizes loans between family and friends. British mogul Richard Branson bought CircleLending this year and relaunched the site in October. Two new sites, Loanio and GlobeFunder, have announced plans to launch in 2008.

"These peer-to-peer lending sites are ideal for people who are not quite in the normal, plain-vanilla credit model that everybody has," says Jim Bruene, publisher of the *Online Banking Report*, a trade publication, and the author of a recent report on social lending. "Certainly business startups or business people who are self-employed fall through the cracks."

No one is counting on social lending to replace banks. Virgin Money has documented $250 million in loans since it was launched as CircleLending in 2001. Prosper users borrowed a total of $103 million through the end of November. The volume is miniscule compared to the total amount loaned: "That's Bank of America (BAC) for a couple hours," Bruene says.

Peer Lending Success

Justin Weeks, co-owner of Royal Oak [Michigan]-based T-shirt company Triple Thread, wanted to expand his two-year-old business but couldn't find a loan from a traditional bank. . . .

"We tried three different banks," he said. "I was looking for $10,000. They would make me go through the whole process, then I would get denied."

Weeks joined the Lending Club, and in about 10 days, he'd gotten $5,000 at a 10.39 percent interest rate, funded by 86 different people.

Nancy Kaffer, "Small Biz Turns to Alternative Lenders,"
Crain's Detroit Business, *November 23, 2008.*

More Flexible Standards

But these sites offer a quick turnaround that appeals to entrepreneurs, especially in a difficult credit market. Nearly one-tenth of responding banks tightened credit standards for small business loans in the third quarter, while none said they had loosened standards, according to the Federal Reserve's October survey of senior loan officers. Social lending sites still evaluate borrowers' credit ratings, but they add another factor as well: the power of the pitch.

Zopa Chief Executive Officer Doug Dolton points to a borrower on his site who got a $10,000 loan at 16.99% to start a Christian comedy club in San Jose. "I think it would have been challenging for him to find that financing from a normal bank," Dolton says. In Zopa's model, the loans are funded by partner credit unions. Then investors on the site can buy certificates of deposit from the credit unions, insured investments that reduce the borrower's payments. "They look at the story and they find the story compelling, and then they click on the borrower," says Dolton. "What we found is that people enjoy reading these stories."

Lending money is still a business, however, and lenders want to see returns regardless of how good a story the borrower has. Lenders are advised to spread their investments across many loans to reduce the risk. "I think that human interest part of it is definitely a factor in how people decide," Bruene says. "Whether it helps this thing go from being a very small niche to being mainstream activity, it's going to depend on whether it works for the lender."

Because peer-to-peer finance sites expose borrowers to thousands of potential lenders rather than just one loan officer, the hope is that some of those lenders will be willing to take on risk that a bank won't.

"Sometimes banks have an inflexible way of operating their credit policy, as they probably should," says Lending Club founder Renaud Laplanche. "Lenders make their own decisions to fund businesses based on different factors: how they relate to that person and how much they want to help that person in addition to getting a good return for themselves."

Lindgren says his creditors on Prosper understood his online business better than bank officers did. "When we went to the banks, they're not used to lending to Internet companies," he says. Loan officers balked at the debt Direct Textbook already had on its books. But the Web-savvy lenders on Prosper understood why the company needed to borrow to buy ads at the back-to-school rush, and they deemed Lindgren a good credit risk because he demonstrated how the ads had led to traffic and sales in the past.

For Lindgren, the loan paid off. Direct Textbook, which expects profits of $120,000 on $500,000 in revenue this year, poured the money into Google ads to boost his site's traffic and the money it makes on sales referrals. "We could pay the full amount back now," Lindgren says. "We keep it open be-cause then that keeps $25,000 in our lines open."

"Prosper's model of 'selfish giving' . . . has as much potential to help people better their lives as does traditional charity."

Peer-to-Peer Lending Offers Citizens the Chance to Help Others

Laura Vanderkam

In this viewpoint, Laura Vanderkam talks about the benefits that peer-to-peer lending sites such as Prosper and Zopa provide to lenders and borrowers. Polls show that many Americans are reluctant to give money to charities because they don't know where their money will go. Peer-to-peer lending sites offer an appealing alternative, Vanderkam asserts, because borrowers must be explicit about how their loans will be used. Lenders on these sites are able to help borrowers improve their lives, while also making some extra money on the interest, she explains. Vanderkam is the author of Grindhopping: Build a Rewarding Career Without Paying Your Dues.

As you read, consider the following questions:

1. According to the Harris Interactive poll, what number of Americans believes charities use funds honestly and ethically?

2. In the author's opinion, what is the danger in giving people money without charging interest?

3. When this article was written, how many of Prosper's loans were three or more months delinquent?

Like many small business owners, Chicago fashion designer Lara Miller, 26, rates "cash flow" as her biggest problem. Recently, it became a crunch. She needed $3,000 to promote her spring/summer 2007 line, but receipts from her previous season's orders hadn't cleared. With no collateral or regular income, she couldn't get a bank loan. . . .

Fortunately, a friend told her about Prosper (www.prosper .com), an online company launched this year [2006] and partly funded by eBay founder Pierre Omidyar. Like eBay, Prosper links people who have something to offer (capital) with people who want something (a loan). Intrigued, Miller set up a profile—that is, she gave Prosper access to her credit report, verified her identity, then explained to potential lenders why she needed the cash. Within a few days, lenders pledging $50–$250 apiece had bid the interest rate on her $3,000 loan down to 9.8% (Prosper bundles these small loans and takes a 1% cut). Miller was on her way.

Microcredit—small loans to people such as Miller who are neglected by traditional banks—is big news these days. Muhammad Yunus, founder of the microcredit Grameen Bank of Bangladesh, accepted the Nobel Peace Prize last week [December 2006] for his work developing the concept. But not all microcredit customers look like Grameen's (Bangladeshis borrowing $100 to buy a cow), and not all microcredit enterprises are charities like Grameen, either.

How I Became a Little-Guy Lender

My first loan was to a bakery in Texas, and I got to feel like an angel investor for $100. . . .

As I got more comfortable lending, I ponied up until I hit $1,500, an amount large enough for diversification but small enough that if something went wrong I wouldn't be sunk. I've now lent to students scraping together tuition, families consolidating credit card debts, entrepreneurs expanding, people hit by major medical costs, and a guy buying an engagement ring. . . .

So far, as long as you discount the hours it has taken to set up my mini-portfolio, I'm doing O.K. . . . If the loans keep paying, it might—just might—be worth it for more than satisfaction of lending a helping hand.

Amy Feldman,
"How I Became a Little-Guy Lender,"
BusinessWeek, *May 5, 2008.*

Between Banks and Charities

Prosper's success in the United States (5,354 loans totaling $25.45 million since February [2006]), and Zopa's, a similar outfit in the United Kingdom, show that microcredit can help people improve their lives in the developed world, too. These companies and the individuals providing microcredit inhabit a unique space between banks and charities—they aim to do good, but also to make a profit. In fact, amid a growing crisis of confidence in U.S. charities, Prosper's model of "selfish giving"—which allows people to make money by giving a hand-up to specific folks who say exactly what they'd do with the cash—has as much potential to help people better their lives as does traditional charity. Before you respond to the annual nonprofit appeals clogging your mailbox this holiday season, you might want to check out some loan listings, too.

Americans will likely give more than $260 billion to U.S. charities this year but many of us aren't sure what this generosity is accomplishing. A recent Harris Interactive poll found that only one in 10 Americans strongly believes charities are honest and ethical in their use of funds. Watchdog group Charity Navigator publishes sobering lists of charities that spend more than 80% of their revenue on fund-raising, and donors often complain that they feel no connection to the end results. As Charity Navigator founder Trent Stamp notes in his blog, "We're one Enron-like scandal away from an entire generation of donors taking their money and going home." That's too bad because plenty of people—even in the United States— need a hand this holiday season. Good, high-paying jobs are hard to come by for people with spotty employment records. Many low-income families are drowning in debt.

Nontraditional Help

The Prosper and Zopa loan models can help in all these situations, often in ways that traditional charities can't. For starters, few nonprofits let you see who will use your cash and for what purpose. The secrecy can make donors feel disconnected. On Prosper, on the other hand, you can hunt through pages of borrowers and choose those with whom you feel a bond.

From the Midwest? You might help an Iowa couple raise $15,000 to make a down payment on a tanning salon. Raised by a single parent? You might help a single mom who's studying to be a nurse practitioner raise $2,500 to consolidate her credit card debts.

Charities also, by definition, can't try to make a buck. But there's a hazard in simply giving people money without charging a profitable interest rate. You'll alleviate suffering, but you might not change the situation.

For-profit microcredit lenders, on the other hand, don't give people capital for kicks. They fund loans only for things that will raise the recipient's income enough that she'll be able to repay her loan. By lowering her interest rate from 30% to 15%, our nurse-to-be will be able to work fewer hours, but she'll still be motivated to finish her courses and start earning the annual $75,000 that the average nurse practitioner makes. A handout wouldn't give her the same ownership. And because the microcredit enterprise makes a profit on her loan, it doesn't need to constantly beg donors for money to make this all happen, an inefficiency that has plagued U.S. charities trying microcredit.

The Risks and Rewards

Of course, unlike giving to charity, helping people on Prosper brings no tax benefits (though few people say this is the driving reason they give to charity). Also, people do occasionally default. To guard against this, Prosper urges lenders to diversify their investments. Of Prosper's 5,354 loans, about 3% are three or more months delinquent.

But charities can waste your money, too, and sometimes banks neglect people just because they're like Miller—no collateral, or in a pinch. With high revenue this season, Miller paid back her $3,000 loan early. Now she plans to borrow $10,000 on Prosper to build an e-commerce site that will take her business to the next level. And she's not the only one coming out ahead. Her lenders will see who they're helping, and they'll make a little bit of money, too. That's not charity—but it feels just as good.

> *"People may be lured by the promise of better rates earned on their money without carefully considering the higher risks of this direct lending."*

Peer-to-Peer Lending Is Often Not Beneficial for Lenders

Michelle Singletary

In this viewpoint, Michelle Singletary argues that while there are many benefits of peer-to-peer lending sites for borrowers, there are more downsides for lenders. First, she says, there are higher default rates on peer-to-peer loans than on bank loans, therefore lenders may not necessarily get their loan money back. In addition, problems often arise from giving loans to family members or friends, which some lending sites facilitate. If people do give loans on peer-to-peer lending sites, they must be realistic and prepared to possibly lose money. Singletary writes the Color of Money, a nationally syndicated column.

As you read, consider the following questions:

1. As the author describes, how does Virgin's business model differ from Prosper's?

Michelle Singletary, "You Can Lend P2P, but Can You Collect?" *Washington Post*, January 13, 2008, p. F1. Copyright © 2008 The Washington Post. Reprinted with permission.

2. What is the top reason consumers cite for getting a peer-to-peer loan?

3. According to Michelle Singletary, what is the best way to pay off old debts?

In the wake of the subprime mortgage meltdown, traditional financial institutions have tightened up on who gets to borrow money. But some people are still finding ways to borrow what they need, thanks to another area of lending that is booming.

Person-to-person lending, or "social" lending, is growing at a phenomenal pace on the Internet as consumers look for an alternate way to pay off debt, according to new research by Javelin Strategy & Research. Javelin predicts that the demand for person-to-person lending services, or P2P, to pay off credit card debt may grow from $38 billion to $159 billion over the next five years.

While many people see opportunities to get cash that might not otherwise be available to them and lenders see a way to deploy some of their extra cash, participants in this emerging form of lending should heed several caveats.

I certainly understand the appeal of utilizing the services of such companies. Often, especially in the current lending market, it's hard if not impossible to get small unsecured loans.

I frequently joke that many people buy a new car not because they want one, but because they can't borrow the $1,500 or $2,000 they need to fix their current vehicle. It's easier to borrow $20,000 for a new car than $1,500 to fix an old one.

Peer Lending Sites

One company seeking to fill the gaps in the private arena is Prosper, an online loan auction site. Prosper works much as eBay does, except instead of people listing consumer items, Prosper brokers consumer and business loans. People who need a loan create a listing for up to $25,000 and set the maximum rate they are willing to pay a lender. People who register as a lender set the minimum interest rate they are willing to earn and bid in increments of $50 to $25,000 on listed loans. Once the auction ends, Prosper takes the bids with the lowest rates and combines them into one loan for the borrower. The company handles all the administration of the loans, including the repayments and, in the case of a default, collection actions.

For its part in the person-to-person lending, Prosper charges a 1 percent to 3 percent loan closing fee. The company also earns money servicing the loans for lenders.

Most recently, Richard Branson's investment firm acquired a majority ownership stake in CircleLending. Branson is the founder and chairman of the Virgin Group. CircleLending has been rebranded Virgin Money USA (www.virginmoneyus .com).

Virgin's business model differs from Prosper in that it helps manage loans only between family and friends. Starting at $99, the company will help put together a promissory note and payment schedule. For additional fees, the company will set up automatic payments, record a lien and service the loan.

Better for Borrowers, Not for Lenders

The top reason consumers said they would use a person-to-person loan is to get a better interest rate. In Javelin's survey, 36 percent of borrowers said they used the service for the better interest rate. Some (33 percent) have turned to P2P to avoid using credit cards. Others (27 percent) go that route because they do not qualify for a loan from a bank or credit union.

Higher-income and younger consumers are the most active users, but Javelin predicts the appeal will widen as the social lending opportunities increase.

Peer Lenders Are Becoming Nervous About Loan Repayment

The average loan amount on Prosper has also fallen 13 percent from last year [2007], as lenders have become nervous about whether borrowers will repay the loan.

Francis A. Vasquez, a 44-year-old lawyer in Vienna, Virginia, who has lent more than $186,000 on the site since January 2007, says one reason for those jitters is the high default rates on the site.

In his first four months on the site last year, for example, Mr. Vasquez said nearly 30 percent of his loans were in default or were four months late, costing him a 1.2 percent loss on his investment. "I don't think there is a whole lot of trust on the site," he said.

Brad Stone, "Lending Alternative Hits Hurdle,"
New York Times, *October 15, 2008.*

Clearly, borrowers benefit from this social lending trend. They can formalize lending agreements and often get a rate better than at a financial institution or pay off higher interest credit card debt. Lenders also get a better rate than they might receive depositing money in a high-yield checking or savings account.

But I see a lot of downsides, as does Jean M. Garascia, an associate analyst with Javelin and author of its report.

"For lenders there is always the issue of default—will someone get paid back," Garascia said.

People may be lured by the promise of better rates earned on their money without carefully considering the higher risks of this direct lending. Even with documentation, the default rate is higher than what financial institutions experience.

And when you add in a personal relationship, lending to a family member or friend can be fraught with problems. Will parents be willing to foreclose on the house where their daughter and grandchildren live?

Responsible Borrowing—and Lending

There's also the issue that people are more often turning to P2P lending to pay off other debts. In experience, it's far better to cut expenses, increase your income or both to pay back consumer debt than to try to borrow more money, even at a lower interest rate. Further, many people are borrowing for things they should be saving for, such as vacation.

If you do consider formalizing a loan with a stranger, relative, or friend by using one of these online services, please heed what Garascia said: "It's important for both lenders and borrowers to be realistic about their finances and be honest about how much they are willing to lend/lose/borrow/afford."

> "One advantage [of peer-to-peer lending sites] is that people often feel a stronger obligation to pay back social loans."

Peer-to-Peer Lending Sites Can Self Regulate

Stacy Teicher Khadaroo

In the following viewpoint, Stacy Teicher Khadaroo, staff writer for the Christian Science Monitor, *explains the recent success of peer-to-peer lending sites. She focuses on a peer-to-peer lending site, GreenNote, which is not regulated by the Securities and Exchange Commission (SEC) and doesn't need to be. Some peer-to-peer lending sites, such as Prosper.com, recently had to stop arranging loans until it registered with the SEC. Khadaroo argues that peer-to-peer lending sites, such as GreenNote, do not need to be regulated by the SEC because they simply help facilitate direct loans between family and friends. More regulation seems unnecessary for the peer-to-peer lending industry, which has been unusually transparent, and is desperately needed during the current credit crunch.*

As you read, consider the following questions:

1. What is an advantage of peer-to-peer lending sites, as stated by the author of this viewpoint, over traditional lending opportunities?

2. According to the viewpoint, why is further regulation from the SEC unnecessary for peer-to-peer lending sites such as GreenNote?

3. What are some peer-to-peer lending sites mentioned in the article that are primarily resources for students?

Christina Christopher was two classes shy of an MBA when DeVry University told her she'd run out of financial aid. She had relied on federal loans, but she hit her limit. With no cosigner for a private loan, she was open to any option she could find.

Someone suggested the Web site GreenNote, which helps students appeal to family and friends for college loans. Within three weeks, she had $2,500 in loans.

She thought GreenNote's 2 percent fee was worth it because the loan process was formalized. "I couldn't just call up [friends] and say, 'Hey, look, this is what I need,'" Ms. Christopher says.

Peer-to-Peer Lending Offers an Alternative to Traditional Lending

As higher-education costs rise and families feel the squeeze on traditional sources for college funding, students are on the hunt for innovative ways to pay their bills. In addition to loan Web sites like GreenNote, other sites are cropping up where students can raise donations for college.

Easy money? What's the catch? Some of the gifts come in exchange for earning good grades or for performing nonprofit volunteer work. And so far, the aura of potential on these sites is much greater than the actual money flow. In the near-term, at least, it appears unlikely that enough donors or lenders will come forward to meet even a fraction of the clamor for cash.

In fact, traffic to peer-lending sites may be driven, in part, by a lack of information about resources available to students and parents, financial-aid experts say. "There's in some cases a false sense that people are unable to get student loans. Usually, the story is not as bad as the headline," says Robert Shireman, executive director of the Project on Student Debt in Berkeley, Calif.

About a quarter of families making between $35,000 and $100,000 didn't even explore a major funding source by filling out the Free Application for Federal Student Aid (FAFSA) in 2007–08, according to a survey by Sallie Mae and Gallup.

If students truly have exhausted federal aid options, it's important to compare interest rates and payback terms before choosing a loan, says Deborah Fox, founder of Fox College Funding, a counseling service in San Diego.

GreenNote has a fixed interest rate of 6.8 percent. This is similar to average federal loan rates and lower than average private rates, which were running about 8.3 percent in early February, according to the Web site Bankrate.com. CEO Akash Agarwal won't share the volume of loans GreenNote has made since it started the lending service last summer, but he says students on average borrow about $5,000 total from two to four lenders. One advantage he touts is that people often feel a stronger obligation to pay back social loans.

"I've decided my repayment is going to be first to Green-Note," says Christopher, who got five loans through the site, primarily from friends of her mother.

Peer-to-Peer Lending Regulation

But peer lending sites are relatively new, and some have been on shaky legal ground of late. Prosper.com recently had to stop arranging loans until it registers with the Securities and

Exchange Commission (SEC), which ruled that it is the seller of securities, since lenders expect a return.

"If someone is wanting to make money off the loan, it's a business relationship," Mr. Shireman says. If the legal issues surrounding the loans aren't properly pinned down, "it's something to be really cautious of."

GreenNote is not registered with the SEC and doesn't need to be, Mr. Agarwal says. Prosper originated loans with a bank and then sold portions of those to loan purchasers, while GreenNote simply helps facilitate direct loans between family and friends, he says.

Gifts are less complicated. At CollegeDegreeFund.com, about 1 in 10 students who have posted profiles have received small gifts—typically ranging from $10 to $100, says cofounder Henner Mohr. Some of the donors are strangers who stumble across the profiles, not just the students' friends.

At GradeFund.com, students as young as 13 can receive education money in exchange for good grades, if they get sponsors. Joel Rojo, a Harvard University sophomore, is starting to pull in gifts for last semester's grades. His older brother pledged $200 for each A.

"It's kind of like that extra little push sometimes if you want to go out at night—or, do you stay in and study? . . . it does give a pretty good incentive," he says.

"The point for us is to get kids involved in their education, and potentially even contributing to paying for it at an earlier age," says Michael Kopko, who cofounded GradeFund .com with brother Matthew.

Mr. Rojo knows the gifts from his six sponsors won't take a big bite out of the roughly $50,000 in debt he expects to incur. "At least it will pay for textbooks or supplies or a new computer—the little essentials we often forget about . . . but they actually do add up," he says.

Nonprofit Peer-to-Peer Lending

Relieving debt burdens and tapping into graduates' interest in community service are the goals behind CharityForDebt.org. College debt "causes the most talented people that have the highest degrees to not be involved with the service-oriented employment in our country," says executive director and co-founder Jonathon Lunardi.

While awaiting official nonprofit status, it's been building up a network of donors, graduates, and nonprofits who could be matched for pilot projects in Dallas and Washington, D.C. Graduates would have their debt paid off at a rate of about $15 for each hour they worked with one of the nonprofit partners. They would submit a weekly portfolio online so the sponsor could see what they'd accomplished.

Finding sponsors is the main challenge for many of these Web sites. At GradeFund.com, for instance, 96 percent of those registered are students, while 4 percent are donors. But hope is not in short supply among these social entrepreneurs and the students drawn to their Web sites.

| *"As much of a headache as regulation can be, it might be what the industry needs to take it to a higher level."*

Government Oversight of Peer-to-Peer Lending Is Not Necessarily Negative

Eileen Ambrose

In the following viewpoint, Baltimore Sun personal finance columnist Eileen Ambrose discusses the Securities and Exchange Commission's (SEC) decision to regulate the peer-to-peer lending industry. While many have highlighted the ways oversight will weaken the industry, Ambrose points out that new regulations will bring many advantages. For instance, oversight will mean greater protections for investors, thus, bringing in more investments. Regulation will also require greater transparency for the industry, she asserts. All of these new requirements will take peer lending companies to the next level, as it has done for Lending Club, which voluntarily registered with the SEC in 2008.

As you read, consider the following questions:

1. How does Eileen Ambrose characterize regulator's rationale for requiring that peer lending companies register with the SEC?

2. Why does Lending Club founder Renaud Laplanche believe his company should be regulated?

3. What does Eric Di Benedetto predict will be the result of regulating the peer lending industry?

Peer-to-peer lending promised to be an alternative to traditional banks and credit cards for small borrowers. But this fledgling industry, which has been operating freely on the Internet, recently has come into regulators' sights.

Regulators argue that some lending sites essentially are selling investments that need to be registered. This has sidelined the largest peer-to-peer lending site, Prosper.com.

The timing couldn't be worse for consumers, with many banks tightening their standards and making it difficult for even some good credit risks to get a loan.

But as much of a headache as regulation can be, it might be what the industry needs to take it to a higher level. Regulation can bring greater transparency and protections for investors who provide the money for loans. And if these investors feel more comfortable, they are more likely to pour money into new loans.

Peer-to-peer lending is only a few years old. These Internet sites match people who need a loan for, say, $1,000 to $25,000, with dozens or hundreds of strangers willing to lend amounts as small as $50. Lending sites act as the go-between, collecting borrowers' payments and forwarding them, along with interest, to the various lenders.

"It's a great idea for the consumer. It's a great idea for the consumer lender," said Jim Bruene, editor of *Online Banking Report*. Borrowers can shop for loans from numerous lenders

SEC Protecting Lenders

The SEC [Securities and Exchange Commission] says it is simply trying to protect the lender-investor, according to Laura Josephs, an assistant director with the commission's enforcement arm who led the case against Prosper. "Generally, we are always cognizant of new companies trying to do something innovative," she says. "It's in nobody's interest to stomp out innovative products."

Jason Del Rey,
"Why Getting a Loan Just Got Harder,"
Inc., January 2009.

without dinging their credit scores, he said. Lenders can reap better returns than with some other investments.

The Regulation Decision's Ripple Effect

San Francisco-based Prosper Marketplace is the biggest player in peer-to-peer lending. Prosper has handled more than $178 million in loans since launching in early 2006. Its site has pictures and stories from consumers explaining why they need money.

But last month [November 2008], the Securities and Exchange Commission [SEC] issued a cease-and-desist order against Prosper, saying it was selling unregistered securities.

According to the SEC, a borrower gets a loan from a bank that Prosper works with. Stakes in that loan, in the form of promissory notes, are then sold to lenders. The notes are investments, the SEC says. Prosper's Web site tells lenders the notes can outperform stocks and money markets, the SEC says.

Prosper suspended making loans and filed to register notes with the SEC and to get approval to create a secondary market.

Regulatory issues have been rippling through the industry.

New York-based Loanio, which launched in October [2008], suspended its activities to undergo registration with regulators.

Lending Club is the only one with regulatory approval. Founder Renaud Laplanche said the company started talking to the SEC a year ago [2007] and concluded that the industry was headed toward regulation. Lending Club began registration with the SEC in April [2008] and finished in early October [2008].

"We are dealing with people's money. It should be regulated," Laplanche says.

California-based Lending Club reopened to new lenders in mid-October [2008] and has attracted more than 3,000, Laplanche says.

It helps that competitor Prosper stopped making new loans just as Lending Club reopened. But Laplanche says lenders see peer-to-peer lending as an attractive alternative to the stock market.

Lenders typically invest $4,000, spread across many loans. After factoring in fees and defaults, investors on average earn 10 percent on their money, Laplanche says.

Lending Club sets the interest rate on loans based on a borrower's creditworthiness. Borrowers must have a credit score of at least 660. The higher the score, the lower the interest rate on the three-year loan. Rates range from 7.237 percent to 20.11 percent.

Bruene, of *Online Banking Report*, says regulation will be a significant barrier to other companies that want to enter peer-to-peer lending, meaning fewer choices for consumers.

But investor Eric Di Benedetto says regulation won't crimp the industry. The Californian has been investing his family's

$1 million in retirement funds with Lending Club since it launched in 2007. Even though his large portfolio of loans had some defaults, he figures his annual return has been about 12 percent.

Di Benedetto sees regulation as a natural next step for the industry.

"It provides an additional level of security and transparency," he says.

He predicts new peer-to-peer sites will continue to crop up, and some of those new entrants might be traditional banks.

Periodical Bibliography

The following articles have been selected to supplement the diverse views presented in this chapter.

Simone Baribeau	"How to Bypass the Bank and Get a Loan," *Christian Science Monitor*, April 30, 2007.
Amy Barrett	"Peer-to-Peer Lending Pain," *BusinessWeek*, April 3, 2009.
Hiawatha Bray	"Need Cash? Just Ask," *Boston Globe*, July 2, 2007.
Kathy Chu	"Peer-to-Peer Lending Hits Its Stride," *USA Today*, December 25, 2007.
Economist	"Crunchless Credit: Peer-to-Peer Lending," October 27, 2007.
Greg Farrell	"Businesses Try to Net Financial Assistance," *USA Today*, April 30, 2008.
Kim Hart	"From the Ground Up," *Washington Post*, August 24, 2008.
Kathy M. Kristof	"Personal Loans, with a Twist," *Los Angeles Times*, August 2, 2009.
Laura Pappano	"Loans in the Time of Facebook," *New York Times*, October 30, 2008.
Rob Walker	"Brother, Can You Spare a Loan?" *New York Times*, May 17, 2009.

CHAPTER 4

Does Microlending Help the Poor?

Chapter Preface

Among the many newer forms of alternative lending that have sprung up in recent decades is microlending, also known as microfinance and microcredit. This type of lending appeared on many people's radar when the man known as its pioneer, Dr. Muhammad Yunus, won the Nobel Prize in 2006. While still relatively novel, the concept of microfinance is actually not as new as many people believe. Yunus founded his microfinance operation, Grameen Bank, in 1983, but the seeds of Grameen were laid a decade earlier.

Muhammad Yunus, an economist, had been teaching at an American university when he decided to return to his home country of Bangladesh in 1972. When that nation was struck by famine in 1974–1975, Yunus said in his book, *Creating a World Without Poverty: Social Business and the Future of Capitalism*, "I wanted to do something immediate to help the people around me get through another day with a little more hope." He began several projects in the village of Jobra, trying to help the villagers become more self-sufficient. "I eventually came face-to-face with poor people's helplessness in finding the tiniest amounts of money to support their efforts to eke out a living," he wrote. In talking with villagers, Yunus learned that they relied on the local moneylender when they needed money to support their small business ventures—one woman made and sold bamboo stools, for instance—but the moneylender's conditions were such that borrowers could never make their way out of poverty.

Yunus first tried to solve the villagers' problem by persuading local banks to lend to them. But bankers were either unwilling to lend to the poor at all, or only willing to test Yunus's ideas on a small sample, never to expand their lending to a larger population. Eventually, "Seeing no prospect of changing the rules of the banks, I decided to create a separate bank for the poor—one that would give loans without collateral, without requiring a credit history, without any legal instruments." In 1983, Grameen Bank was born.

Since Grameen's founding, hundreds—perhaps thousands—of other microfinance companies have followed suit. In December 2007, *Forbes* compiled a list of the top 50 microfinance companies from a total of 641 companies; many more companies did not respond to requests for information. As the landscape of microfinance has expanded, it has also evolved. For example, in recent years, the profit margins of microfinance companies have attracted big banks, and now such multinational firms as Citigroup and Morgan Stanley are investing in microfinance. The profitability of microfinance is one of many issues that are frequently debated. For example, considering that the initial vision of microcredit was to help the poor, how much should microfinance companies profit? Beyond this, the extent to which microcredit actually eliminates poverty is also a frequent topic of debate and is explored in this chapter. The viewpoint authors also address the impact of microcredit on gender equity and economic development. As microfinance continues to expand and transform, understanding and engaging in the debates surrounding this innovative form of lending become more and more critical.

| *"All that is required to get poor people out of poverty is for us to create an enabling environment for them."*

Microloan Programs Help the Poor Achieve Self-Sufficiency

Muhammad Yunus

Muhammad Yunus is an economist who developed the concept of microcredit and founded Grameen Bank based on that idea. He was awarded the Nobel Peace Prize in 2006. In the following viewpoint, he explains how microcredit differs from the mainstream banking system, in which policies have historically excluded the poor. He argues that microcredit has more potential to help the poor than other charity or economic development programs because it encourages individuals to tap their implicit entrepreneurial energy and drive, and gives them the tools to build a more sustainable way of life.

As you read, consider the following questions:

1. What result does Muhammad Yunus say was predicted by those who warned him against lending money to the poor?

Muhammad Yunus, *Creating a World Without Poverty: Social Business and the Future of Capitalism.* New York: Public Affairs, 2007. Copyright © 2007 by Muhammad Yunus. All rights reserved. Reprinted by permission of Public Affairs, a member of Perseus Books Group.

2. According to Yunus, what assumption about entrepreneurship pervades standard economic thinking?

3. Why does Yunus believe that lending money to women has greater benefits than lending to men?

Grameen Bank started very small and grew slowly. What was revolutionary about it was the shift in thinking it represented.

In the past, financial institutions always asked themselves, "Are the poor credit-worthy?" and always answered no. As a result, the poor were simply ignored and left out of the financial system, as if they didn't exist. I reversed the question: "Are the banks people-worthy?" When I discovered they were not, I realized it was time to create a new kind of bank.

None of us like the idea of apartheid. We object when we hear about such a system in any form, anywhere. We all understand that no one should suffer because he or she happened to be born in a certain race, class, or economic condition. But our financial institutions have created a worldwide system of apartheid without anyone being horrified by it. If you don't have collateral, you are not credit-worthy. To the banks, you are not acceptable on our side of the world.

Imagine if the global electronic communications system of the banking world suddenly collapsed and every financial institution in the world suddenly stopped functioning. Banks everywhere would shut their doors. ATM screens would go blank. Credit and debit cards would no longer work. And billions of families would be unable even to put groceries on the table. Well, this is exactly the situation that half of the world's population lives with every day—a nonstop horror story.

If the poor are to get the chance to lift themselves out of poverty, it's up to us to remove the institutional barriers we've created around them. We must remove the absurd rules and laws we have made that treat the poor as nonentities. And we must come up with new ways to recognize a person by his or her own worth, not by artificial measuring sticks imposed by a biased system.

The problem I discovered in Bangladesh—the exclusion of the poor from the benefits of the financial system—is not restricted only to the poorest countries of the world. It exists worldwide. Even in the richest country in the world, many people are not considered credit-worthy and are therefore ineligible to participate fully in the economic system.

Not Just a Third World Problem

In 1994, I received a letter from a young woman, Tami, in Hixon, Texas, a writer working for a newspaper. Tami wrote to me about her adventures in trying to do business with the American banking system:

> When I was a child trying to open a simple savings account, I was put off by the bank's demand that I produce two pieces of photo identification. What would a child be doing with photo ID in the first place?
>
> My experiences as an adult have not been better.
>
> My mother just received a $500 money order refund from the U.S. government to pay her back for a money order the post office had lost. She took it to the bank we were using the day we went to close out our account. They refused to cash it for her because, as they said, "You no longer have an account here." She had to take it to one of the many check-cashing companies that have sprung up in the United States in recent years, and we were shocked when they took twenty percent—$100!—as the fee for cashing it.
>
> I started checking into these places and found that many people are forced to use them, mainly elderly people who live on Social Security checks and the working poor who cannot establish bank accounts because they cannot keep

minimum balances, afford per-check charges and service charges, or show the bank that they already have good credit. Some people have trouble providing I.D. to banks to open accounts. It's hard enough to show them the I.D. they require to cash a check.

At the newspaper where I worked, I received a paycheck every week. I always took it to the very bank it was drawn on and always to one of the same two tellers. Every week they insisted on seeing my driver's license and as if having a state-issued license with my photograph on it was not enough, demanded to see a credit card too. Presumably if I am in debt, I must be honest.

Isn't it outrageous that low-income people who are struggling to make ends meet are the ones who have to pay *the most* for basic financial services—when they can get access to those services at all?

Exploiting the Poor

In the years since I heard from Tami, the problem has not improved. New ways to exploit the poor are always being invented. For example, if you are a member of the middle class, you may never have heard of payday loans, small, short-term loans, usually for less than $1,500, that are given to low-income Americans who don't have access to mainstream sources of credit. They use these loans to get from one payday and the next—to pay an unexpected doctor's bill or fix a car or a broken appliance when money runs short.

Middle- and upper-income individuals would use a credit card to cover such expenses. If the credit card bill is paid in full and on time, no finance charge would be assessed. If it takes a few months to pay the bill, an annualized interest rate in the neighborhood of 25 percent might be charged. But the working poor, who don't qualify for a conventional credit card, are forced to take payday loans instead. And the fees and interest charges for these loans can come to an annual rate of 250 percent, or even higher.

It is so tempting to blame the poor for the problems they face. But when we look at the institutions we have created and how they fail to serve the poor, we see that those institutions and the backward thinking they represent must bear much of the blame.

A New Kind of Bank

At Grameen Bank, we challenged the financial apartheid. We dared to give the poorest people bank credit. We included destitute women who had never in their lives even touched any money. We defied the rules. At each step along the way, everybody shouted at us, "You are wasting your money! The money you lend will never come back. Even if your system is working now, it will collapse in no time. It will explode and disappear."

But Grameen Bank neither exploded nor disappeared. Instead, it expanded and reached more and more people. Today, it gives loans to over seven million poor people, 97 percent of whom are women, in 78,000 villages in Bangladesh.

Since it opened, the bank has given out loans totaling the equivalent of $6 billion (U.S.). The repayment rate is currently 98.6 percent. Grameen Bank routinely makes a profit, just as any well-managed bank should do. Financially, it is self-reliant and has not taken donor money since 1995. Deposits and other resources of Grameen Bank today amount to 156 percent of all outstanding loans. The bank has been profitable every year of its existence except 1983, 1991, and 1992. And most significant of all, according to Grameen Bank's internal survey, 64 percent of our borrowers who have been with the bank for five years or more have crossed the poverty line.

Grameen Bank was born as a tiny homegrown project run with the help of several of my students, all local girls and boys. Three of them are still with me in Grameen Bank, after all these years, as its leading executives.

More Economic Blind Spots

Simply being willing to extend credit to the poor was a revolutionary step in terms of conventional economic thinking. It meant ignoring the traditional belief that loans cannot be made without collateral. This assumption, which the vast majority of bankers hold without analyzing it, questioning it, or even thinking about it, in effect writes off half the human race as being unworthy to participate in the financial system.

Viewed more broadly, however, the Grameen Bank system also involves rethinking many other assumptions in mainstream economics. I have already discussed the fact that economic theory sketches a radically oversimplified image of human nature, assuming that all people are motivated purely by the desire to maximize profit. It only takes a few seconds of thought about the people we all know in the real world to realize that this is simply untrue. And this is only one of the many blind spots of conventional economic theory that Grameen Bank has had to overcome.

A second is the assumption that the solution to poverty lies in creating employment for all—that the only way to help the poor is by giving them jobs. This assumption shapes the kinds of development policies that economists recommend and that governments and aid agencies pursue. Donor money is poured into massive projects, mostly government run. Private capital is invested in big enterprises that are supposed to jump-start local and regional economies, employing thousands of people and turning the poor into affluent taxpayers. It is a nice theory—except that experience shows that it doesn't work because the necessary supportive conditions don't exist.

Economists are wedded to this approach to alleviating poverty because the only kind of employment that most economics textbooks recognize is wage employment. The textbook world is made up solely of "firms" and "farms" that hire different quantities of labor at various wage levels. There is no room in the economic literature for people making a living

Other Microcredit Companies Follow Grameen Bank's Example

A young American couple, Matthew and Jessica Flannery, founded Kiva after they worked in Africa and realized that a major impediment to economic development was the unavailability of credit at any reasonable cost.

"I believe the real solutions to poverty alleviation hinge on bringing capitalism and business to areas where there wasn't business or where it wasn't efficient," Mr. Flannery said. He added: "This doesn't have to be charity."

Nicholas Kristof,
"You, Too, Can Be a Banker to the Poor,"
New York Times, *March 27, 2007.*

through self-employment, finding ways to develop goods or services that they sell directly to those who need them. But in the real world, that's what you see the poor doing everywhere.

Working Versus Having Jobs

An American friend recently visited Bangladesh for the first time. After traveling through one of the poorest areas in our country, he wrote me:

> In the United States, I associate rural poverty with apparent absence of economic activity. I'm thinking of the scenes my wife and I have observed when driving through the depressed counties of upstate New York—deserted downtown areas, storefront windows with just a few tired old articles on display, shuttered offices and factories, and so on. You can drive all day through these communities, scarcely ever see a soul, and arrive at your destination utterly baffled as to how anyone there makes a living. (And of course fewer and

fewer people in those counties can make a living these days, which is why many of them have moved to the city.)

But the tiny slice of rural Bangladesh that I saw today, while far poorer (in monetary terms) than any place in New York, is an incredible beehive of economic activity. Every village has its shopping street where dozens of tin-roofed sheds jostle one another, piled high with goods for sale (shoes, medicines, furniture, clothing, DVDs, foodstuffs—you name it) or offering services from barbering to tailoring. On the back roads, the villagers offer their wares spread out on mats—baskets, hats, rounds of bread, a few potatoes or vegetables. And in practically every house or yard you pass, you see people at work, making or fixing or preparing things for trade—tending milk cows, carving wooden furniture, soldering jewelry, gathering crops.

The villagers my American friend observed do not have "jobs" that conventional economists would recognize. But they are working hard, producing income, feeding their families, and trying to lift themselves out of poverty. What they lack is the economic tools they need to make their work as productive as possible.

At Grameen Bank, I have tried to demonstrate that credit for the poor can create self-employment and generate income for them. By not recognizing the household as a production unit and self-employment as a natural way for people to make a living, the economic literature has missed out on an essential feature of economic reality. I am not arguing against creating jobs. Go full speed ahead on that. But don't assume that people must wait for jobs to materialize, and that self-employment is merely a temporary stopgap. People should have options to choose from, including both jobs and self-employment. Let people choose what suits them. Many people do both.

This mistake is linked to another blind spot in standard economic thinking: the assumption that "entrepreneurship" is a rare quality. According to the textbooks, only a handful of people have the talent to spot business opportunities and the courage to risk their resources in developing those opportunities.

On the contrary, my observations among the poorest people of the world suggest—and decades of experience by Grameen Bank and other institutions confirm—that entrepreneurial ability is practically universal. Almost everyone has the talent to recognize opportunities around them. And when they are given the tools to transform those opportunities into reality, almost everyone is eager to do so.

Provide a Prosperous Base

To me, the poor are like bonsai trees. When you plant the best seed of the tallest tree in a six-inch-deep flower pot, you get a perfect replica of the tallest tree, but it is only inches tall. There is nothing wrong with the seed you planted; only the soil-base you provided was inadequate.

Poor people are bonsai people. There is nothing wrong with their seeds. Only society never gave them a base to grow on. All that is required to get poor people out of poverty is for us to create an enabling environment for them. Once the poor are allowed [to] unleash their energy and creativity, poverty will disappear very quickly.

Economic theory has other blind spots as well. Read most economic textbooks and you will never encounter any such thing as a "man," a "woman," or a "child." As far as economists are concerned, none of these things exist. The closest they come to acknowledging the existence of human beings is when they talk about "labor"—a collection of robot-like beings whose only mission in life is to work for factory owners, office owners, or farm owners. And since economic theory doesn't recognize that "labor" is made up of both men and women, its view of the world is male-dominated (treating "male" as the "default value" between male and female).

When challenged, economists defend this retreat into extreme abstraction by saying they do it for the sake of "simplicity." I understand that sometimes it is necessary to simplify in order to see things clearly. But when "simplification" means ignoring essentials, it goes too far. Albert Einstein has been quoted as saying, "Everything should be made as simple as possible, but not simpler than that." Mainstream economics makes everything "too simple," and therefore it misses reality.

Human Beings Are Not Labor Units

At Grameen Bank, we quickly discovered that, in the real world, it is important to think about men, women, and children not as units of "labor" but as human beings with varying capacities and needs. Observing the actual behavior of the people we lent money to, we soon found that giving credit to poor women brings more benefits to a family than giving it to men. When men make money, they tend to spend it on themselves, but when women make money, they bring benefits to the whole family, particularly the children. Thus, lending to women creates a cascading effect that brings social benefits as well as economic benefits to the whole family and ultimately to the entire community. At Grameen Bank, we discovered the mother first. Then we discovered the children—not through any emotional or moral compulsion, but for sound economic reasons. If poverty is to be reduced or eliminated, the next generation must be our focus. We must prepare them to peel off all the signs and stigmas of poverty, and instill in them a sense of human dignity and hope for the future.

So any program addressed to children should not be looked upon as a "humanitarian" or "charitable" program. In reality, it is a prime development program—no less so (and much more so, I would argue) than building an airport, a factory, or highways.

And this leads to yet another major blind spot in conventional economics: the focus, in development strategy, on material accumulation and achievement. This focus needs to be shifted to human beings, their initiative and enterprise.

The first and foremost task of development is to turn on the engine of creativity inside each person. Any program that merely meets the physical needs of a poor person or even provides a job is not a true development program unless it leads to the unfolding of his or her creative energy.

This is why Grameen Bank offers the poor not handouts or grants but credit—loans they must repay, with interest, through their own productive work. This dynamic makes Grameen Bank sustainable. Loan repayments supply funds for future loans, to the same individuals or to new bank members, in an ever-expanding cycle of economic growth. It also helps the poor demonstrate to themselves that they can change their world for the better—and it gives them the tools to do just that, for themselves.

Critics often say that microcredit does not contribute significantly to economic development. Are they correct? I think the answer depends on how you define "economic development." Is it measured by income per capita? Consumption per capita? Or anything per capita?

To me, the essence of development is changing the quality of life of the bottom half of the population. And that quality is not to be defined just by the size of the consumption basket. It must also include the enabling environment that lets individuals explore their own creative potential. This is more important than any mere measure of income or consumption.

Microcredit turns on the economic engines among the rejected population of society. Once a large number of these tiny engines start working, the stage is set for big things.

> *"The way to realize the promise of microcredit is to embed the best features of the model within a broader development strategy for promoting growth, decent employment, and poverty reduction."*

Microcredit Has a Limited Capacity for Ending Global Poverty

Robert Pollin

Robert Pollin is a professor of economics at the University of Massachusetts-Amherst and the author of several books. In this viewpoint, he argues that while microcredit has certainly done some good in developing countries, its potential impact on global poverty is severely limited. Pollin argues that this is especially true in countries dominated by neoliberalist policies, which tend to perpetuate economic inequality. To make a serious dent in eliminating poverty, developing countries need to provide additional support for the poor such as better infrastructure and more jobs.

As you read, consider the following questions:

1. According to Robert Pollin, what has been Grameen Bank's most important advance?

2. How does Pollin describe the "developmental state" economic model?

3. Why are many Kenyans starved for credit, in Pollin's view?

How effective is microcredit as a poverty-fighting tool? In 1976, Muhammad Yunus, the 2006 Nobel Peace Prize winner, launched the pioneering institution in the field, the Grameen Bank in Bangladesh. The industry's growth has been explosive since Grameen opened its doors. According to a recent story in the *Economist*, "there are now some 10,000 microfinance institutions lending an average of less than $300 to 40 million poor borrowers worldwide." These institutions have made important advances relative to the array of moneylenders and pawnbrokers that had previously controlled the provisioning of banking services to the world's poor.

At the same time, considered on [their] own, Grameen-style initiatives have limited capacity to fight global poverty, especially when placed in a policy setting dominated by neoliberalism. Neoliberalism became the ascendant economic model throughout the developing world in the late 1970s, at roughly the same time that the Grameen Bank began operations. The main tenets of neoliberalism include macroeconomic policies focused on eliminating inflation rather than expanding job opportunities; cutting government subsidies—including credit subsidies—and related systems of support for domestic businesses, including microenterprises; and opening domestic markets to imports, multinational investors and speculative financiers. These policies in developing countries have produced slower economic growth, increasing inequality, and no progress in reducing poverty—that is, an insurmountable headwind countering the efforts of the Grameen Bank and its confederates.

How the Grameen Model Works

Regardless of the larger policy issues, the Grameen model has made undeniable contributions in bringing financial services to poor people. The first contribution is the simple recognition that credit and related services—including bank accounts and insurance policies—can be important resources for advancing the well-being of the poor, just as they are with everyone else. The second is in targeting women as loan recipients, empowering the women within their families and helping them to sustain their home-based microenterprises.

Grameen's most important advance has been to develop an alternative to traditional collateral as a basis for lending to the poor. Under a traditional system, you can't obtain a loan until you have sufficient assets to surrender to the bank, moneylender, or pawnbroker in the event that you fail to make loan repayments. But poor people, by definition, have few assets to pledge—perhaps a few livestock animals, a small plot of land, or jewelry. Losing these few assets to a creditor would likely bring destitution. Grameen's innovation was to create borrowing groups, typically of five women. Each group member could receive loans only as long as everyone made payments. This promotes both mutual support among group members as well as peer pressure to keep up with payments. It also created opportunities for large numbers of poor people to become creditworthy for the first time.

High Interest Rates

Counteracting these positive innovations, the average lending rates by Grameen and other microfinance institutions far exceed standard measures of affordability. Real annual interest rates (i.e., after controlling for inflation) on group loans range between 30–50%, according to a 2004 survey in *MicroBanking Bulletin*. These rates are perhaps lower than what moneylenders typically charge, but remain punishingly high. Imagine a working class family in the United States taking out a $100,000 mortgage to purchase a home, then having to pay $30–50,000 per year in interest alone in order to keep their home. Defenders of such arrangements in the microfinance world contend that, accounting for the risks to the lender, these rates are appropriate; and that anything less will not attract profit-seeking bankers into this market. According to this approach, microfinance can only reach its full global potential—lifting out of poverty the more than 1 billion people of the world now living on roughly $1/day—if it can attract profit-seekers into the business, not just aid agencies and private do-gooders.

In addition, the Grameen Bank has long prided itself on maintaining repayment rates as high as 95%. However, the accuracy of these figures has been disputed, including in a careful *Wall Street Journal* report in 2001. Some observers contend that, in fact, Grameen allows distressed borrowers to roll over or stretch out their repayments rather than declaring them in default. This may well be the most effective and humane approach under the circumstances. But again, it is clearly inconsistent with the hard-nosed business model supported by an increasing share of microfinance enthusiasts.

Context Is Everything

But whether the credit terms are low or high, microenterprises run by poor people cannot be broadly successful simply because they have increased opportunities to borrow money. For large numbers of microenterprises to be successful, they also need access to decent roads and affordable means of moving their products to markets. They need marketing support to reach customers. They need a vibrant, well-functioning domestic market itself that encompasses enough people with enough money to buy what these enterprises have to sell. Finally, microbusinesses benefit greatly from an expanding supply of decent wage-paying jobs in their local economies. This is the single best way of maintaining a vibrant domestic market. In addition, when the wage-paying job market is strong, it means that the number of people trying to survive as microentrepreneurs falls. This reduces competition among microbusinesses and thereby improves the chances that any given microenterprise will succeed.

These additional measures for supporting microenterprises—a decent transportation infrastructure, support in marketing the products of microenterprises, a high level of domestic demand, and an abundance of decent wage-earning jobs—have all been closely associated with what used to be termed the "developmental state" economic model. Different versions of the developmental state model—including state socialism, import-substituting industrialization, and the East Asian state-directed economies—prevailed in developing countries for the first 30 years after World War II, before these models were overtaken by neoliberalism. Each of these developmental state models encountered serious problems. But on balance they all achieved successes in promoting economic growth and greater equality. This is in contrast with the neoliberal record of declining average growth rates and rising inequality.

Development Banks

One of the key institutions of the developmental state model that was largely dismantled under neoliberalism is the state-directed development bank. State-directed development banks provided cheap, long-term credit for domestic businesses that enabled these businesses to develop their productive and marketing capabilities at a sustainable pace. The MIT [Massachusetts Institute of Technology] development economist Alice Amsden concludes in her major study *The Rise of the Rest: Challenges to the West from Late-Industrializing Economies*:

Microloans Can't Undo the Effects of Neoliberalist Policies

Grameen [Bank] loans cannot address poverty's structural causes. For example, today's rural poverty in Mexico, a typical case, can be traced to explicit acts. Opening Mexico to cheap, subsidized U.S. corn has killed internal markets, impoverishing villages. Loosening collective "ejido" control of the land has dispossessed communities of this source of income as the wealthy buy it up. Privatizing utilities and lowering spending on education and farm support have deepened desperation. Individual entrepreneurship and marketing, mostly in the informal economy, cannot undo such policies of neoliberal globalization.

Betsy Bowman and Bob Stone, "Can Grameen Bank-Style Microcredit Eliminate Poverty?" Center for Global Justice, March 2007. www.globaljusticecenter.org.

"From the viewpoint of long-term capital supply for public and private investment, development banks ... were of overwhelming importance." Amsden documents this in the cases of Mexico, Chile, Korea, Brazil, and Indonesia. Amsden also points out that the government's role in providing subsidized long-term credit was substantial even in developing countries where development banks themselves were of relatively minor importance. These cases included Malaysia, Thailand, Taiwan, and Turkey.

It is true that, in the countries that Amsden cites, the subsidized credit went to large-scale enterprises focused on breaking into export markets. But the general approach can also be adapted to dramatically expand the availability of affordable credit to small and microenterprises producing primarily for domestic markets.

A Proposal for Kenya

A good case study of how this might be done is Kenya, where, under the auspices of the International Poverty Centre of the UN [United Nations] Development Programme, two colleagues and I are working on an "employment-targeted" development model that gives prominence to issues of credit access for the poor. At present, Kenya already has a widespread system of microfinance institutions in place. Its commercial banking system is also generally well-developed.

Despite this, Kenyan farmers, small formal businesses and informal microenterprises are starved for credit. This is because commercial banks do not generally lend to these sectors while the microfinance institutions themselves do not have sufficient resources to provide large-scale funds.

The solution seems straightforward: to bring into much closer alliance the formal commercial banking system and the microfinance institutions. Our proposal is to inject a major pool of subsidized credit equal to roughly 20% of total private investment in Kenya. These funds would be made available to commercial banks on condition that they in turn make loans to the microfinance institutions. The microlenders will be far more adept than the traditional commercial banks at making loans to small businesses, informal enterprises, and agricultural small holders.

A Different Framework for Microcredit

We propose that government guarantees be set at 75% of the total amount of loans that commercial banks make to microfinance institutions. This will enable interest rates to fall dramatically—specifically by the amount at which the loan is being guaranteed and the bank's risk is correspondingly reduced. This means that, with a 75% government loan guarantee, if the market rate for a microcredit loan was 40%, the subsidized rate would be 10%. This would make the loan affordable for borrowers while still maintaining market incentives for lenders. The creative methods of establishing eligibility for loans pioneered by the Grameen Bank could be applied effectively within this framework.

Even assuming default rates on these guaranteed loans as high as 30%, the total cost to the Kenyan government of paying off the guaranteed portion of the loans to creditors would be no more than about 5% of its total fiscal budget. This is a relatively small price for creating credit access for the poor throughout the country at interest rates 75% below market rates.

This example suggests that the way to realize the promise of microcredit is to embed the best features of the model within a broader developmental strategy for promoting growth, decent employment, and poverty reduction. Operating within the context of a neoliberal policy framework, microcredit initiatives will continue to face overwhelming obstacles in fighting global poverty.

| "Microloans make poor borrowers better off. But, on their own, they often don't do much to make poor countries richer."

Microloans Do Not Encourage the Economic Growth That Developing Countries Need

James Surowiecki

In the following viewpoint, James Surowiecki writes that while microloans help individual citizens, on the whole, they don't do enough to make developing countries richer. Because the loans are generally very small, and are given to small businesses with only one paid employee, they rarely generate more jobs. What poor countries need most, Surowiecki argues, is more small to medium companies that will produce jobs on a large scale. The hype over microlending has distracted people from solutions that might actually transform developing countries, he says. Surowiecki writes the Financial Page, a business column in the New Yorker.

As you read, consider the following questions:

1. According to James Surowiecki, what is the "idealized view" of microfinance?

2. In Surowiecki's view, why is the entrepreneurship rate in Peru higher than in the United States?

3. How does the author characterize the "missing middle" phenomenon?

Making loans and fighting poverty are normally two of the least glamorous pursuits around, but put the two together and you have an economic innovation that has become not just popular but downright chic. The innovation—microfinance—involves making small loans to poor entrepreneurs, usually in developing countries. It has been around since the nineteen-seventies, but in the past few years it has seized the imaginations of economists, activists, and bankers alike. The U.N. [United Nations] declared 2005 the International Year of Microcredit, and the microfinance pioneer Muhammad Yunus won the Nobel Peace Prize in 2006, while celebrities like Natalie Portman and companies like Benetton have become fervent microloan advocates. Even ordinary Americans can now get in on the act, at sites like Kiva.org, where you can make a microloan yourself. (Right now [2008], a clothing vender in Cambodia needs seven hundred dollars to "purchase more clothes to sell.")

This vogue has translated into a flood of real dollars: Institutional and individual investments in microfinance more than doubled between 2004 and 2006, to $4.4 billion, and the total volume of loans made has risen to $25 billion, according to Deutsche Bank. Unfortunately, it has also translated into a flood of hype. There's no doubt that microfinance does a tremendous amount of good, yet there are also real limits to what it can accomplish. Microloans make poor borrowers better off. But, on their own, they often don't do much to make poor countries richer.

Microloans Don't Generate the Jobs That Developing Countries Need

This isn't because microloans don't work; it's because of how they work. The idealized view of microfinance is that budding entrepreneurs use the loans to start and grow businesses—expanding operations, boosting inventory, and so on. The reality is more complicated. Microloans are often used to "smooth consumption"—tiding a borrower over in times of crisis. They're also, as Karol Boudreaux and Tyler Cowen point out in a recent paper, often used for nonbusiness expenses such as a child's education. It's less common to find them used to fund major business expansions or to hire new employees. In part, this is because the loans can be very small—frequently as little as fifty or a hundred dollars—and generally come with very high interest rates, often above thirty or forty percent. But it's also because most microbusinesses aren't looking to take on more workers. The vast majority have only one paid employee: the owner. As the economist Jonathan Morduch has put it, microfinance "rarely generates new jobs for others."

This matters, because businesses that can generate jobs for others are the best hope of any country trying to put a serious dent in its poverty rate. Sustained economic growth requires companies that can make big investments—building a factory, say—and that can exploit the economies of scale that make workers more productive and, ultimately, richer. Microfinance evangelists sometimes make it sound as if, in an ideal world, everyone would own his own business. "All people are entrepreneurs," Muhammad Yunus has said. But in any successful economy most people aren't entrepreneurs—they make a living by working for someone else. Just fourteen percent of Americans, for instance, are running (or trying to run) their own business. That percentage is much higher in developing countries—in Peru, it's almost forty percent. That's not because Peruvians are more entrepreneurial. It's because they don't have other options.

The "Missing Middle"

What poor countries need most, then, is not more microbusinesses. They need more small- to medium-sized enterprises,

Microfinance Alone Does Not Bring Economic Development

Economic development does wonders for peace, but what does microfinanced entrepreneurship really do for economic development? Can turning more beggars into basket weavers make Bangladesh less of a, well, basket case? A few small port cities or petro-states aside, there is no historical precedent for sustained improvements in living standards without broad-based modernization and widespread improvements in productivity brought about by [more] dynamic entrepreneurship.

Amar Bhidé and Carl Schramm, "Phelps's Prize,"
Wall Street Journal, *January 29, 2007.*

the kind that are bigger than a fruit stand but smaller than a Fortune 1000 corporation. In high-income countries, these companies create more than sixty percent of all jobs, but in the developing world they're relatively rare, thanks to a lack of institutions able to provide them with the capital they need. It's easy for really big companies in poor countries to tap the markets for funding, and now, because of microfinance, it's possible for really small enterprises to get money, too. But the companies in between find it hard. It's a phenomenon that has been dubbed the "missing middle."

The problem is a dearth not just of lenders but also of people willing to buy an ownership stake in companies, like the angel investors and venture capitalists that American entrepreneurs often rely on. Microfinance has led us to focus on lending, but it can be hard for young companies to get big purely on bank loans, which consume cash flow that could be reinvested in the business. Supplying the missing middle will require backers who want to invest in companies rather than just lend to them. There's been some progress on this front of late; three weeks ago [February 19, 2008], Google.org, the Soros Economic Development Fund [SEDF], and the Omidyar Network announced that they are setting up a firm in India that will invest only in small to medium businesses. But there have yet to be celebrities speaking up for the missing middle.

Microloans Do Good—but Not Enough

Both socially and economically, microloans do a lot of good, working what Boudreaux and Cowen call "Micromagic." But the overselling of their promise has made us neglect the enterprises that could be real engines of macromagic. The cult of the entrepreneur that the microfinance boom has helped foster is understandably appealing. But thinking that everyone is, and should be, an entrepreneur leads us to underrate the virtues of larger businesses and of the income that a steady job can provide. To be sure, for some people the best route out of poverty will be a bank loan. But for most it's going to be something much simpler: a regular paycheck.

> "Microfinance often targets women and, hence, if well managed, has the potential to make a significant contribution to gender equality and promote sustainable livelihoods."

Microloans Empower Poor Women and Enhance Gender Equity

Zarina Geloo

In the following viewpoint, Zarina Geloo discusses the impact that microcredit programs have had on poor women in Africa. These programs generally make more loans to women and, thus, not only help to diminish poverty, but also serve to empower women by giving them the resources they need to support themselves. When women are no longer economically dependent on their husbands, they become more self-sufficient and less vulnerable to abuse by men. Geloo is the editor of the Guardian Weekly *in Zambia.*

As you read, consider the following questions:

1. What percentage of the world's poor are women, according to the International Labour Organization (ILO)?

2. How might microcredit programs impact HIV infection rates in women, in the Society for Women and AIDS in Zambia's (SWAAZ) view?

3. What are the two kinds of poverty to which Emily Sikazwe refers?

Since 2000, microcredit institutions have been mushrooming in Africa, resulting in many success stories of poverty reduction among many women on the continent. It is hoped that through campaigning for microcredit, more than 175 million vulnerable and disadvantaged women will be able to access credit for self-employment and other business services by the end of 2015.

According to Juan Somavía, director-general of the International Labour Organization (ILO), "Microcredit plays a critical role in empowering women—it helps deliver newfound respect, independence, and participation for women in their communities and their households."

Microfinance is the provision of financial services to the poor in a sustainable way, and utilises credit, savings, and other products to help families take advantage of non-risky income-generating activities.

According to the ILO, 70 percent of the world's poor are women, and yet, traditionally, women have been disadvantaged in access to credit and other financial services; but microfinance often targets women and, hence, if well managed, has the potential to make a significant contribution to gender equality and promote sustainable livelihoods.

On the ground, women like Professor Nkandu Luo of Zambia are championing the cause for more economic empowerment for vulnerable African women.

"We want women to be empowered financially so that they can make decisions about their lives, and stop the abuse that comes with being economically powerless, but we also want the empowerment to be total," she tells *New African Woman*.

Rebuilding Minds

She believes that for women to develop a deeper sense of self, they must rebuild their minds and believe that they are not just beings that belong to anybody. They need to know that they enter marriages as an equal partner and they should be treated with respect. And in order to provide better for their families and communities, they need to be able to look after themselves and be healthy. They also need to have a strong voice in all aspects of their lives. Young girls should be socialised differently, to be independent rather than subservient, and to look at themselves as important beings in their own right. Women also have to see their own talent and harness it, to turn into a resource.

These are some of the principle premises of the motivational Society for Women and AIDS in Zambia (SWAAZ), which is spearheaded by Prof Luo, a former health minister and member of Parliament.

SWAAZ is also concerned about how to reduce the incidences of HIV infection in women and its argument is that women [could] negotiate safer sex practices if they were not financially dependent on men. With financial and economic freedom, they would not engage in risky sexual practices and abuse. However, Prof Luo is quick to stress helping women to make money is not enough: "It is only a part of the equation, it needs to go with a total awareness and appreciation of being a human being with rights, as a person who has something worthwhile to contribute to the family, community and nation," she tells *New African Woman*.

A Better Standard of Living

This is a slow process and entails a mind-set change, as women have been socialised to be unquestioning and subservient, as exemplified here by Beti Nachali's story.

Like many African women, Nachali became totally dependent on her husband when she got married. She worked their field in Isoka, northern Zambia, to provide some food. However, when things got tough, even the little food they had was sold to buy other essentials or to pay school fees. In addition, even though Nachali was the main breadwinner from the yield she produced, she, however, had no say on when to sell the harvest or what items were essential. Her husband did not feel it was her place to know and she knew not to argue.

All that changed, however, when SWAAZ visited her village in Bbuzi and began talking about empowerment for women. The organisation gave the women a grant and asked them to form a group and come up with income-generating activities. Nachali's group has not looked back since.

"We engage in baking, knitting and sewing; I have expanded my field. We were given start-up funds and are running profitably. Our families are better off, children are in schools, and people eat more frequent meals. We are not rich, and we do not have huge surpluses, but we definitely have a better standard of living," says Nachali.

No Longer Powerless

Like the other women in her group, Nachali says financial freedom, however little, is a great boon to their psyche. "When we began to earn money independently, we felt powerful, to the extent that we were able to stand in front of the headmaster and demand to negotiate for a staggering of the school fees for those that had fallen behind in payments. It's something that had bothered us women in the village but we had never done anything about it because we felt so powerless," she adds.

Enabling Women to Catch Up

It is a known fact that most formal financial institutions do not serve the poor (the bulk of who[m] are women) because of perceived risks, lack of physical collateral, and low or non-profitability of enterprises.

As a result, poor women continue to wallow in poverty because they lack access to credit facilities.

Only microfinance packages come to their rescue.

Microfinance projects that target women enable them to "catch up" in the economic world.

AfricaNews,
"Zimbabwe: Microfinance Key to Women's Empowerment,"
February 14, 2007.

Her husband Abdanon explains it more practically. He thought that his wife earning her own money would make her 'stubborn', 'big headed' and 'disrespectful'. He feared being emasculated by having a financially independent wife. He acknowledges that the power many men use over their wives is about money. "He who holds the purse strings holds the torch," he translates a local proverb. Abdanon always felt that he was the absolute head of his household, accountable only to himself, and that his wife was his property. But he now agrees that apart from more income being generated by his wife, she has also learnt to be more confident and they now work as a team, discussing family matters and making decisions together.

Women Work Toward Equality

Nachali says when she increased her vegetable production her husband got excited and wanted to 'help' her by selling the produce and dreaming up ideas about what he would do with the money. He balked when she said she would accompany him to the market and also when she demanded that she has a say in how the money was to be spent. He didn't take it well at first and assured her she would fail. "I have not failed. See the socks my husband is wearing? I bought them," she says proudly. Though seemingly trivial, her pride in this simple gesture can only be appreciated when one considers that, a year ago, Nachali could not even make the simple decision to buy something as mundane as a pair of socks without consulting her husband.

There are today hundreds of other examples similar to Nachali's across Africa, where, of all the efforts to reduce women's poverty, microcredit is the new buzz word.

For example, single parent Judith Kwalonga got a $1,000 loan to start a small tuck shop in the market from a women's credit institution three years ago. She now has three food stalls. She makes about $500 each month—not a lot of money by Western standards—but in a country where the monthly food basket is about $200 and 80 percent of the population live on less than a dollar a day, she admittedly is doing well.

"I think microcredit is very good; from where I am standing I cannot think of any better way to help women," she says.

Two Kinds of Poverty

There are similar success stories that women tell about microcredit. But Emily Sikazwe, executive director of Women for Change in Zambia, advises caution. "Women can earn as much money as is possible, but it will not necessarily change their lives, as they could still be tools of their families. They will still use the income for children and husbands and take nothing for themselves. They will, in effect, still be poor."

Like Luo, Sikazwe says it's not just about creating wealthy; empowering women is dealing with two kinds of poverty: poverty of the mind and poverty of material things.

"Both men and women must see how wrong the picture is when there is an imbalance in workload. For example, why is it acceptable for men to cut wood using appropriate tools and transport it using a scotch cart, but women use inappropriate tools and have to carry wood on their heads? This is poverty of the mind. People must recognise that there is something wrong with this picture and make amends," she says.

Women Must Take Charge of Their Lives

Women for Change encourages communities to form associations and gives them resources to start income-generating activities. Beatrice Hangoma, who is chairperson of one such association, says there is also a follow-on effect which is bigger than wealth creation.

"With women actively engaged in income-generation activities, there is a vibrancy in the communities that comes from not just having enough to eat, but also a sense of self-worth. It is not just the initial grants that create wealth for women, it is what they do after the start-up.

"It is really difficult to put in words how one feels—to come from a situation where you are so poor and helpless, to a place where you are strong, not because you have a bit of financial independence, which is good itself, but because you realise you actually can control your life."

She adds however: "Whether women are empowered through microfinancing, grants or donations, what will determine their success is the change of mind-set, from being passive, shouldering the burden of poverty on their own to women who can take charge of their lives."

> "The evidence on microcredit and women's empowerment is ambiguous. Access to credit is not the sole determinant of women's power and autonomy."

Microloans Do Not Necessarily Enhance Gender Equity

Susan F. Feiner and Drucilla K. Barker

Susan F. Feiner is professor of economics and women's studies at the University of Southern Maine. Drucilla K. Barker is professor of economics and women's studies at Hollins University. In the following viewpoint, the authors dispute claims that microcredit programs diminish poverty and empower women. In fact, they say that microcredit programs go nowhere near the actual roots of poverty. These programs cannot single-handedly empower women either, since lack of access to credit is not the only impediment to gender equality. Feiner and Barker conclude that microcredit programs tend to encourage women to work in the informal sector, which has historically kept women overworked and underpaid.

As you read, consider the following questions:

1. According to the authors, what is the neoliberals' solution to poverty?

2. How might microloans given to women increase conflict within their households, in the authors' view?

3. What do the authors propose as a more effective solution to helping women escape poverty?

The key to understanding why Grameen Bank founder and CEO [chief executive officer] Muhammad Yunus won the Nobel Peace Prize [in 2006] lies in the current fascination with individualistic myths of wealth and poverty. Many policy makers believe that poverty is "simply" a problem of individual behavior. By rejecting the notion that poverty has structural causes, they deny the need for collective responses. In fact, according to this tough-love view, broad-based civic commitments to increase employment or provide income supports only make matters worse: Helping the poor is pernicious because such aid undermines the incentive for hard work. This ideology is part and parcel of neoliberalism.

For neoliberals the solution to poverty is getting the poor to work harder, get educated, have fewer children, and act more responsibly. Markets reward those who help themselves, and women, who comprise the vast majority of microcredit borrowers, are no exception. Neoliberals champion the Grameen Bank and similar efforts precisely because microcredit programs do not change the structural conditions of globalization—such as loss of land rights, privatization of essential public services, or cutbacks in health and education spending—that reproduce poverty among women in developing nations.

The Microcredit Approach

What exactly is microcredit? Yunus, a Bangladeshi banker and economist, pioneered the idea of setting up a bank to make loans to the "poorest of the poor." The term "microcredit" reflects the very small size of the loans, often less than $100. Recognizing that the lack of collateral was often a barrier to borrowing by the poor, Yunus founded the Grameen Bank in the 1970s to make loans in areas of severe rural poverty where there were often no alternatives to what we would call loan sharks.

His solution to these problems was twofold. First, Grameen Bank would hire agents to travel the countryside on a regular schedule, making loans and collecting loan repayments. Second, only women belonging to Grameen's "loan circles" would be eligible for loans. If one woman in a loan circle did not meet her obligations, the others in the circle would either be ineligible for future loans or be held responsible for repayment of her loan. In this way the collective liability of the group served as collateral.

The Grameen Bank toasts its successes: Not only do loan repayment rates approach 95%, the poor, empowered by their investments, are not dependent on "handouts." Microcredit advocates see these programs as a solution to poverty because poor women can generate income by using the borrowed funds to start small-scale enterprises, often home-based handicraft production. But these enterprises are almost all in the informal sector, which is fiercely competitive and typically unregulated, in other words, outside the range of any laws that protect workers or ensure their rights. Not surprisingly, women comprise the majority of workers in the informal economy and are heavily represented at the bottom of its already low income scale.

Perpetuating the Gender Division of Labor

Women and men have different experiences with work and entrepreneurship because a gender division of labor in most cultures assigns men to paid work outside the home and women to unpaid labor in the home. Consequently, women's

Microfinance Focus on Women Diminishing

A landmark study released on Thursday [April 17, 2008] by Women's World Banking (WWB), a network of microfinance institutions in 29 countries ... examined what happened at 27 outfits as they morphed from nongovernmental (typically not-for-profit) organizations [NGOs] into regulated financial institutions, and found that they often end up lending to a smaller percentage of women—the very people they often started to help.

Barbara Kiviat,
"Microfinance: Women Being Cheated?"
TIME, *April 17, 2008.*

paid work is constrained by domestic responsibilities. They either work part-time, or they combine paid and unpaid work by working at home. Microcredit encourages women to work at home doing piecework: sewing garments, weaving rugs, assembling toys and electronic components. Home workers—mostly women and children—often work long hours for very poor pay in hazardous conditions, with no legal protections. As progressive journalist Gina Neff has noted, encouraging the growth of the informal sector sounds like advice from one of [author Charles] Dickens's more objectionable characters.

Why then do national governments and international organizations promote microcredit, thereby encouraging women's work in the informal sector? As an antipoverty program, microcredit fits nicely with the prevailing ideology that defines poverty as an individual problem and that shifts responsibility for addressing it away from government policy makers and multilateral bank managers onto the backs of poor women.

A Boon for Lenders, Not Necessarily for Borrowers

Microcredit programs do nothing to change the structural conditions that create poverty. But microcredit has been a success for the many banks that have adopted it. Of course, lending to the poor has long been a lucrative enterprise. Pawnshops, finance companies, payday loan operations, and loan sharks charge high interest rates precisely because poor people are often desperate for cash and lack access to formal credit networks. According to Sheryl Nance-Nash, a correspondent for Women's eNews, "the interest rates on microfinance vary between 25% to 50%." She notes that these rates "are much lower than informal moneylenders, where rates may exceed 10% per month." It is important for the poor to have access to credit on relatively reasonable terms. Still, microcredit lenders are reaping the rewards of extraordinarily high repayment rates on loans that are still at somewhat above-market interest rates.

Anecdotal accounts can easily overstate the concrete gains to borrowers from microcredit. For example, widely cited research by the Canadian International Development Agency (CIDA) reports that, "Women in particular face significant barriers to achieving sustained increases in income and improving their status, and require complementary support in other areas, such as training, marketing, literacy, social mobilization, and other financial services (e.g., consumption loans, savings)." The report goes on to conclude that most borrowers realize only very small gains, and that the poorest borrowers benefit the least. CIDA also found little relationship between loan repayment and business success.

Inconclusive Evidence of Women's Empowerment

However large or small their income gains, poor women are widely believed to find empowerment in access to microcredit loans. According to the World Bank, for instance, microcredit empowers women by giving them more control over household assets and resources, more autonomy and decision making power, and greater access to participation in public life. This defense of microcredit stands or falls with individual success stories featuring women using their loans to start some sort of small-scale enterprise, perhaps renting a stall in the local market or buying a sewing machine to assemble piece goods. There is no doubt that when they succeed, women and their families are better off than they were before they became microdebtors.

But the evidence on microcredit and women's empowerment is ambiguous. Access to credit is not the sole determinant of women's power and autonomy. Credit may, for example, increase women's dual burden of market and household labor. It may also increase conflict within the household if men, rather than women, control how loan moneys are used. Moreover, the group pressure over repayment in Grameen's loan circles can just as easily create conflict among women as build solidarity.

Grameen Bank founder Muhammad Yunus won the Nobel Peace Prize because his approach to banking reinforces the neoliberal view that individual behavior is the source of poverty and the neoliberal agenda of restricting state aid to the most vulnerable when and where the need for government assistance is most acute. Progressives working in poor communities around the world disagree. They argue that poverty is structural, so the solutions to poverty must focus not on adjusting the conditions of individuals but on building structures of inclusion. Expanding the state sector to provide the rudiments of a working social infrastructure is, therefore, a far more effective way to help women escape or avoid poverty. Do the activities of the Grameen Bank and other microlenders romanticize individual struggles to escape poverty? Yes. Do these programs help some women "pull themselves up by the bootstraps"? Yes. Will microenterprises in the informal sector contribute to ending world poverty? Not a chance.

> *"EnComún aims to offer economic options that keep people in Mexico."*

Microlending in Mexico Enables Poor Citizens to Stay in Their Home Country

Lourdes Medrano

In this viewpoint, Arizona Daily Star reporter Lourdes Medrano discusses the effects that microlending has had on poor towns in Mexico. Many individuals and families that might have migrated to the United States—perhaps illegally—are instead staying in Mexico because of the opportunities offered by microlending programs such as EnComún, Medrano asserts. These programs typically lend more to women, who can then support themselves and their families if they are single, or supplement their husbands' incomes, while still maintaining their households.

As you read, consider the following questions:

1. How does the concept of "communal risk" work, as Medrano explains it?

2. What is EnComún's current repayment rate, according to the program director?

3. What is EnComún's rationale for focusing on female borrowers?

Desperate for rent money, Yadira Marquez recently tried to push her husband north of the border illegally in search of higher-paying work.

But instead of bidding farewell to the father of her three children, Marquez came across a program that extends small loans to entrepreneurs too poor to qualify for a regular bank loan. The $200 that she borrowed from EnComún de la Frontera two months ago allowed her to invest in silver jewelry, which she sells door to door. Her husband, Armando Figueroa, kept his $80-a-week job at a local *maquila*—one of the city's many U.S.-owned factories.

"This loan by no means has solved all our financial problems," said Marquez, 33. "But with my earnings I'm able to supplement my husband's salary and pay for all of our children's school-related expenses."

She is one of about 1,500 Nogales [Sonora, Mexico] residents participating in the microcredit program known in the U.S. as BanComún de la Frontera.

Modeled on a successful practice in Bangladesh, the program aims to increase the economic self-sufficiency of needy Mexicans—particularly women.

Despite being minute, the low-interest loans—which range from $50 to $800 per person—are making a difference in the city's poorest neighborhoods, said program director José Carlos Mendoza Escoto.

EnComún works largely because borrowers take on a communal risk, he said. Each entrepreneur becomes part of a group responsible for ensuring that all its members are on track with payments that include 3.5 percent monthly interest. If one person defaults, no member receives another loan.

After some initial missteps, the program's repayment rate has climbed to about 95 percent, Mendoza Escoto said. Adjustments were made to target a diversified clientele in a border area where the risk of migration is high, he added.

Offering Economic Options

By focusing on female entrepreneurs, he said, the program builds on evidence that shows women are more likely than men to repay loans and use business profits to improve overall family life.

"Most of our clients, about 85 percent, are women," Mendoza Escoto noted. "They are enterprising women and heads of household who are eager to get ahead."

In some cases, the director said, the women are single, or married with absent husbands, including some who have migrated across the U.S. border.

It may be too early to gauge what impact the program may have on illegal immigration, Mendoza Escoto said. But he noted that EnComún aims to offer economic options that keep people in Mexico.

"We would like them to be able to see that the fruits of their own labor can allow for a life of dignity here," the director said of the mostly home-based entrepreneurs—a vital part of Mexico's commerce.

EnComún's borrowers sell everything from tacos and tamales to shoes and washing machine covers.

The program began as BanComún in 2003 with just a few borrowers as a pilot project of Catholic Relief Services and BorderLinks, a Tucson group that offers border education. It later became its own nonprofit entity, known as EnComún in Mexico for legal reasons. Its board of directors includes members from both sides of the border, including representatives from BorderLinks and the Catholic relief agency.

A Rare Opportunity

Since its inception, the program has pulled in about $2.2 million from various public and private sources, said Erica Dahl-Bredine, manager for Catholic Relief Services' Mexico program. The funding includes about $420,000 from the U.S Agency for International Development [USAID] and $1.5 million from Howard Buffett, the son of billionaire Warren Buffett.

Dahl-Bredine said plans are in the works to seek loans from the Mexican government.

The existing funding has made possible a recent expansion into Ciudad Juárez, Chihuahua, she said. Next up is an office in Agua Prieta and the creation of a social investment fund that will allow people to help finance the socioeconomic welfare of EnComún clients.

"We are not so pretentious to think that this program will stop poverty," she said. "But we do hope that people's standard of living can improve."

EnComún is a rare economic opportunity in Yadira Marquez's impoverished Colonia Colosio, born some years ago after squatters invaded the area, divvied up plots and set up a shantytown of old cardboard boxes, tarpaper and discarded wood pieces. Many are cinder block houses now, but Marquez and her family live in one of the original structures.

Marquez leaves her neighborhood often to sell her bracelets, necklaces, and rings. On a good week, Marquez said she can surpass her husband's factory salary. Her profits usually cover her children's school expenses, Marquez said, but she also must set aside money for a loan payment every two weeks at a meeting with her 14-member group of borrowers. Except for one, the 11 women and 3 men all live in the same colonia.

Working Together

Every other Tuesday, Marquez walks down a dusty dirt road to neighbor Veronica Arizmendi's home for the group's regu-

Keeping Mexican Workers at Home

Mexicans in the United States send home as much as $25 billion in remittances each year; and ... more is now being used to start local microcredit banks. The hope, of course, is that fostering new, job-creating businesses at home will eventually keep Mexican workers at home.

That ideal is being borne out in a small but growing numbers of rural Mexican towns, especially in the country's backward south ... Earlier this year [2007] I visited one of them, Santa Cruz Mixtepec, an indigenous Mixtec community in the rugged mountains of southern Oaxaca. Two-thirds of Santa Cruz's 3,000 residents live undocumented *al otro lado*, "on the other side" in the United States; and each year they send back almost $1 million. A few years ago the wives in Santa Cruz took a chunk of that money and founded a microcredit bank, Xu Nuu Ndavi (Mixtec for "Poor People's Money"). With starter loans of $5,000 and up, Xu Nuu Ndavi has helped build businesses as diverse as furniture-making and tomato greenhouses ...

Slowly but surely, Xu Nuu Ndavi is yielding the most important result: Santa Cruz's workers are starting to return to *este lado*, or "this side," and some who considered leaving have decided to stay.

Tim Padgett, "It Starts in Mexico,"
America, October 15, 2007.

lar morning meeting. Last week, she was fined $2 for being tardy. An absence costs group members another $2; failure to bring along a payment card results in a $1 fine.

During the last meeting in Arizmendi's small living room, the group collected payments from all but one member. She promised to bring Arizmendi, the group's treasurer, her share as soon as she got her factory paycheck later in the week. The woman, who invested her loan money in a tortilla-making operation, is the only member from outside the neighborhood.

Arizmendi, 26, worries when a member falls behind because that means the group has to cover the missing payment. It's only happened once, she said, and the member later got caught up.

"I don't want anything to hurt our credit," said Arizmendi, who with her $200 loan added stock to the tiny market she opened next to her kitchen about a year ago. She plans to take out a second loan to tear down walls and expand her closet-sized *abarrotes* as soon as she pays off the first one in July [2007].

Making ends meet still is a struggle, said Arizmendi, who until recently was a single mother of two working illegally as a store sales clerk just over the border in Nogales, Arizona.

Selling sodas, fruit, chips and school supplies out of her home while her new husband drives delivery trucks allows Arizmendi to stay close to her two children at all times.

"It's hard because I take care of the store alone," she said. "But the business is growing slowly, and Yami will be able to start helping soon," she said of her 7-year-old daughter. Her son, Antonio, is 10 months old.

Making a Better Living

A knock on the store window interrupted Arizmendi. Regular customers Andrés Alejandro Malmaceda, 6, and Mario Cota Meléndrez, 5, wanted to trade their *pesos* for candy and bananas. Bounty in hand, the boys happily sauntered away, oblivious to the poverty around them.

A few miles away, Heberto Coronado tended to a diminutive restaurant that he and his wife, Carmen González, opened a month ago near the baseball stadium. Puesto América seats just eight customers, but Coronado said he plans to expand with profits derived from the couple's weekend sales of food and clothing at the *tianguis*, a street market. Coronado recently quit his longtime factory job to focus on the family business.

"It's more work, but one of the benefits is that you're working for yourself, and if you work hard, you can make a better living," Coronado said.

His only waitress, Maria Esther Lizardo Hernandez, has received $600 in loans from EnComún in the past year. She invested the money in new clothing that she sells at the street market on weekends.

Her profits have allowed her to buy a used car that makes the job easier, the mother of one said. Her business also enables her to contribute to her growing family's budget.

"Sometimes I make more than my husband," she noted.

At 22, Lizardo Hernández is reaching for a dream.

"My goal is to open a boutique downtown," she said, sounding confident.

| *"Along the road to previously unavail-*
| *able financing, some Mexicans are*
| *stumbling badly."*

Microlending in Mexico Makes Many Poor Citizens Even Poorer

Keith Epstein and Geri Smith

Keith Epstein is a BusinessWeek *Washington bureau correspondent. Geri Smith is the* BusinessWeek *Mexico bureau chief. In the following viewpoint, Epstein and Smith examine the negative effects of microloans given to poor citizens by large banks in Mexico. While the average interest rate of nonprofit microlending institutions worldwide is 31 percent, the authors explain, for-profit banks in Mexico, where there are no legal limits, charge 50 percent to 120 percent. As a result, many financially unsophisticated borrowers become trapped in a cycle of debt, and wind up even poorer than they were before.*

As you read, consider the following questions:

1. What reason accounts for the success of Azteca's business model, besides the lack of government regulation, according to the authors?

2. How do Elektra clerks earn the biggest commission, according to Keith Epstein and Geri Smith?

3. According to Chuck Waterfield, what APR does Azteca's average interest rate translate to?

In a gleaming office tower in Mexico City secured with retinal scanners, bulletproof glass, and armed guards, dozens of workers in white lab coats dart around a large operations center monitoring long rows of computers. Along one wall, 54 enormous screens flicker dizzyingly with numbers, graphs, and fever charts: a relentless stream of data. You'd think the urgent mission involved tracking the trajectory of a spacecraft or the workings of a national power grid, not tiny amounts of cash and credit for Mexico's working poor.

The transactions are so minuscule they hardly seem worth the bother. The average loan amounts to $257. But for Banco Azteca, a swiftly growing bank affiliated with Latin America's largest household retailer, the small sums represent a torrent of revenue that has caught even its founders by surprise. For three decades, microlending was seen as a tool of nonprofit economic development. Now poor people are turning into one of the world's least likely sources of untapped profit, primarily because they will pay interest rates most Americans would consider outrageous, if not usurious.

With no legal limits on interest levels and little government oversight, for-profit banks in Mexico impose annual interest rates on poor borrowers that typically range from 50% to 120%. That compares with a worldwide average of 31% among nonprofit microlending institutions, and the 22% to 29% that Americans with bad credit histories incur on credit card debt. Azteca's business model succeeds not only because it can charge credit-starved clients almost whatever it wants. Equally important is that low-income Mexicans anxious about maintaining their reputation tend to pay back what they owe, regardless of the hardship. Those who slip behind receive frequent visits from motorcycle-riding collection agents. Default rates are infinitesimal. "We lend to them as much as they can borrow," says Azteca Vice-Chairman Luis Niño de Rivera, "and they can borrow as much as they can pay."

Whiff of Profits

In a Mexico that is modernizing economically even as most people still struggle to make ends meet, Azteca has discovered an improbable market for financial services. Much larger companies based in the U.S. and Europe also have picked up the whiff of profits. Wal-Mart, which obtained a Mexican banking license a year ago, began offering loans for purchases at 16 of its 997 Mexican outlets in November. In the U.S., the retailer markets itself as a friend to the budget-conscious. In Mexico, it charges interest rates that might set off popular and political revolts back home, although Wal-Mart describes its terms as appropriate to the Mexican market. At one store west of Mexico City, a 32-inch LG plasma TV with a price tag of $957 can ultimately cost as much as $1,474, thanks to a 52-week payment plan that carries an annual percentage rate (APR) of 86%.

Banamex, Mexico's second-largest bank and a wholly owned unit of Citigroup, is stepping up its pitches of personal loans to the working poor in 127 cities where it operates shops called Crédito Familiar, or Family Credit. HSBC Holdings last year bought a 20% stake in Financiera Independencia, a high-interest consumer lender that went public on Nov. 1. The Swiss insurer Zurich Financial Services is underwriting term life insurance policies that are sold along with small loans in Mexico. And homegrown nonprofit Compartamos morphed into a full-fledged commercial bank last year; it went public in April, reaping hundreds of millions of dollars for investors. All are examples of how financial players worldwide are pursuing profits by putting loans within reach of deprived borrowers.

Access to credit opens opportunities for the poor. But it creates tempting hazards as well, which in Mexico are drawing many unsophisticated families into a maze of debts. Pawnshops and loan sharks, whose interest rates of up to 300% have plagued generations of Mexicans, now face rivals offering terms that are less harsh. But along the road to previously unavailable financing, some Mexicans are stumbling badly.

The Arana family is but a blip on one of the wide screens at Azteca's operations center. Beneath the digital glimmer lies a story of striving. Adrián Arana Sánchez, his wife, Francisca, and their extended family take whatever work they can find, adding a few pesos here and there. Last July, Adrián lost an $80-a-week job delivering soft drinks to stores in gritty, exhaust-choked San Martín Texmelucan, a city of 143,000 two hours southeast of Mexico City. He now brings home half that amount peddling vegetables door to door and making plaster-cast statuettes of Jesus. Francisca sells crunchy slices of jicama root outside an elementary school. With four children, two grandchildren, and a son-in-law, they live in a four-room cinder block house in the shadow of snow-capped volcanoes once revered by the Aztecs.

Although indigent by U.S. or Western European standards, the Aranas see themselves as aspiring consumers and even as entrepreneurs in a society that makes all manner of goods and services available for what seem like manageable weekly payments. Banco Azteca plays a central role in that emerging credit economy. Started five years ago, it operates from the nearly 800 locations of its parent, Grupo Elektra, Latin America's largest electronics and home appliance chain. Elektra/Azteca has the sort of ubiquitous presence that Wal-Mart enjoys in the U.S.

Seeking a Middle-Class Life

The dazzling yellow facades of Elektra/Azteca outlets shout for attention in rundown neighborhoods. Inside the store across from the Catholic cathedral in San Martín Texmelucan, a tag on a six-speaker sound system throbbing with *ranchero* music carries a price of $691, but larger bold print stresses weekly payments of only $16. An installment plan can be arranged by Azteca staffers who work from metal desks at the back. Over 18 months, the weekly payments nearly double the price, to $1,248. That's an APR of 88%. APR is commonly used in the U.S. to compare total loan costs. In Mexico, Azteca isn't legally obliged to disclose it—and doesn't. (Mexican loans include a 15% tax on financial services.)

Adrián Arana, 50 years old and with a sixth-grade education, has become a regular customer at this branch of Elektra/Azteca. He and Francisca, who completed only the second grade, have obtained a series of small loans over the past four years to purchase a CD player, bicycle, TV, video camera, and bedroom furniture. In 2006 they took the next step, borrowing $920 to pursue a long-cherished ambition: opening a dry goods store in the front room of their house. They saw the store as a means to achieve stability, and maybe a middle-class life. But like many tiny businesses started by inexperienced proprietors, this one soon failed. A neighbor had just opened a similar but better-stocked home shop. The Aranas toiled diligently at their other jobs to pay back the loan, missing some weekly payments and incurring late fees. With an APR of 105%, the loan ended up costing about $1,485 over a year. But they paid it off.

Determined to try again, they were back at Azteca in February with a new plan, this time to start a gift shop. Azteca granted them a bigger loan, for $1,380 over 18 months, but deducted $65 up front, leaving the Aranas with $1,315 and an APR of 90%. They say they didn't understand these terms. They focused instead on the weekly payment of only $32. "They never tell you what the interest rate is," says Adrián. "They say, 'Sign here,' but they don't give you time to read everything."

Some Azteca executives concede that borrowers sometimes walk away confused. "Terms are explained to them, maybe not as clearly as they should be, but many clients don't understand," says Pedro Morales, head of the bank's local legal department. "They take on financial commitments they can't meet." But Niño de Rivera, the bank's vice-chairman, says: "There is no pressure to sign loans, and consumers are encouraged to shop around freely for what best suits their needs."

The Aranas used the $1,315 to buy picture frames, toys, and inexpensive cosmetics, which they displayed in their front room, beneath a dangling lightbulb illuminating a portrait of the Virgin of Guadalupe. Once again, their business faltered. Two textile factories in the area had closed recently, throwing thousands out of work. Mexico offers no government benefits to cushion such adversity. The Aranas saw few customers.

For six months they made their payments, but then, in July, Adrián lost his soft drink delivery job. By September, past due notices and interest charges were piling up, and an Azteca collection agent was visiting regularly. "We either eat or we pay off the loan," says Adrián. The despairing family resorted to borrowing $200 from a loan shark at 10% a month. Informal lending of this sort, despite its attendant threat of violence, is not prohibited in Mexico. Azteca's local collections chief, Alejandro Tejeda, says it's a shame that borrowers can land in such trouble. "But these people made a commitment, and they need to live up to it," he says.

With no money to pay the loan shark or Azteca, and fearing that the bank will seize their few belongings, the Aranas are trying to sell their house. So far they haven't found a buyer, and if they do, it's not clear where they would live. They're keeping food on the table, barely, with Adrián's door-to-door sales of tomatoes and herbs, which he transports in the basket of a large tricycle. "We never thought this would happen," he says. "We're sinking fast."

Banco Azteca and Grupo Elektra are key parts of Grupo Salinas, an amalgam of media, telecommunications, and retail businesses controlled by billionaire Ricardo B. Salinas Pliego. A maverick among Mexico's business elite, he has sparked controversy. In 2006 he settled civil fraud allegations by the U.S. Securities and Exchange Commission concerning the finances of his TV network, then traded on the New York Stock Exchange. He denied wrongdoing but paid $7.5 million and was barred for five years from serving as an executive or director of companies listed in the U.S.

The Salinas family began selling furniture on credit more than a century ago in the northern city of Monterrey. Ricardo, 51, says he learned early in life that those who work in Mexico's informal economy, without pay stubs or much collateral, and who can't afford sofas or blenders outright, will snap up merchandise if offered seemingly manageable terms. "If you want to become rich, sell to the poor," he recalls his grandfather instructing him.

He learned to get even richer by lending to the poor, and to those who are better off. Azteca targets 14.5 million Mexican families earning $5,100 to $33,600 a year. Mexico has a total population of 109 million, with a median annual household income of $7,297. Mainstream Mexican banks cater to the wealthier elite, while less than one-third of working-poor families have access to any banking services at all.

Azteca has absorbed Elektra's ethos of high-pressure employee quotas and incentives. Elektra clerks, clothed in the store's signature bright yellow, earn commissions on top of their standard weekly salary of $120 for tacking on extras, such as warranties, life insurance, and even long-distance bus tickets. The biggest score comes from persuading a customer to spread payments over the longest possible period, 104 weeks. "Sell on credit and earn much more money!" an online company training manual states.

How Much Profit Is Too Much

Compartamos is more efficient than other Mexican microfinance institutions and its own borrowing costs are lower, thanks to its strong credit rating. Critics charge that it has not passed those savings on to its customers.

The numbers seem to bear that out. A study last year [2007] by the Consultative Group to Assist the Poor, known as CGAP, a microfinance industry group based at the World Bank, estimated that 23.6 percent of Compartamos's interest income went to profits. Its return on average equity is more than triple the 15 percent average for Mexican commercial banks.

Profit is not a dirty word in the microfinance world. The question is how much is appropriate. CGAP estimates the average return on assets for self-sufficient organizations to be 5.5 percent. The figure for Compartamos was 19.6 percent in the fourth quarter.

Elisabeth Malkin,
"Microfinance's Success Sets Off a Debate in Mexico,"
New York Times, *April 5, 2008.*

Motorbike Cavalry

The strategy has far exceeded the expectations of Grupo Elektra executives. The bank already contributes one-fifth of its parent's $5 billion in annual revenue. It boasts a consumer loan portfolio of $2 billion and a healthy 22.3% return on shareholder equity.

The main Elektra/Azteca branch in San Martín Texmelucan aims to meet a daily target of $9,000 in fresh loans. The money isn't spewed out carelessly. With efficiency unusual in the Mexican marketplace, the bank deploys a cavalry of credit and collection agents on motorbikes. These *jefes de crédito y cobranza* visit borrowers within 24 hours of a purchase or loan application.

Juan Carlos Pérez Lopanzi, a 25-year-old college graduate who studied international commerce, serves as one of 13 credit agents in San Martín Texmelucan. One October morning, he rumbles up to the home of Maria Teresa Hernández as neighbors peer from their windows. Hernández, a 50-year-old street vendor, wants to borrow $460 for a new hot dog wagon. She isn't home, so Lopanzi questions her adult daughter about the family's finances. Do they rent or own? Have they lived there at least two years? What do they spend on food?

With each answer, Lopanzi taps the screen of a handheld computer. Data will be routed to Azteca's operations center in Mexico City. The state-of-the-art system keeps the cost of processing 7 million transactions a day to a mere 3 cents per transaction, according to Azteca. "It's amazing—all this is for poor people," says Juan Arévalo Carranza, the bank's technology chief.

Back in dusty San Martín Texmelucan, Azteca's proprietary software alerts the agent, Lopanzi, that Hernández, who earns $276 a month, doesn't qualify for a $460 loan. He offers $370 instead. That will require $10.60 weekly payments for 12 months for an APR of 85%. Hernández will end up paying $551. "If she had more income, she could have a shorter payback period, and the interest rate would be lower," the agent explains to the daughter. She shrugs, then nods in acceptance.

"Tell her she can go by the store this afternoon for her check," Lopanzi says, as he registers the serial numbers of the daughter's stereo, DVD player, TV, and refrigerator. The items' resale value, preprogrammed into Lopanzi's digital device, must add up to around double the value of the loan. If the woman fails to pay, Azteca will cart away the daughter's possessions and sell them in a Grupo Elektra used goods store.

Azteca deducts the depreciated value of seized goods from outstanding loan balances, so if someone who doesn't pay has enough possessions to cover the debt, the bank considers it paid. Azteca bars such customers from borrowing again but doesn't count them as having defaulted, which helps explain its stated loan failure rate of just 1%. Banks serving more prosperous clients average a 5.3% default rate on consumer loans.

Mexican lenders benefit from attitudes cultivated in a society lacking a welfare safety net, personal bankruptcy system, or meaningful consumer protection laws. Credit bureaus have recently sprung up in Mexico, including one that Elektra helped start in 2005, and many among the working poor worry about sullying their new credit ratings. They assume that, one way or the other, they or their relatives will just have to pay back whatever they borrow, says Gustavo A. Del Angel, an economic historian who studies microfinance at the Center for Research and Teaching in Economics in Mexico City

"Bad Manners"

Borrowers who fall behind realistically fear public embarrassment. Photocopies of debtors' national identification cards sometimes turn up on telephone poles and at central marketplaces with warnings that say "DON'T LEND TO THIS PERSON!" Six months ago, an Azteca agent in San Martín Texmelucan posted such flyers. The company fired him.

"Our system is not intended to be publicly shaming," says Niño de Rivera, Azteca's vice-chairman, but he acknowledges it "is intended to exercise peer pressure."

Even as Mexico's economy modernizes, companies operate with minimal oversight from government. Luis Pazos, head of Condusef, Mexico's regulator of consumer financial transactions, says his agency logs complaints about Azteca's collection methods and the adequacy of its disclosure of credit terms. "We've talked with that bank about the bad manners they've had," he says. But Condusef hasn't taken any substantial action against Azteca, which says it scrupulously polices the behavior of its employees. Last year, in a brash move characteristic of Grupo Salinas, lawyers for Azteca went to court rather than comply with a new law requiring banks to inform clients of the total financing costs they are charged. Azteca sought a type of protective order with which individuals or companies can shield themselves from application of a particular law or other government action. A federal judge granted the exception.

Freed of disclosure requirements, Azteca continues stressing weekly payments rather than long-term interest rates. When pressed for its average annual rate, Azteca asserts that it is about 55%. But Chuck Waterfield, a consultant based in Lancaster, Pa., who specializes in financial modeling for microlenders, points out that if Azteca's average rate is translated to make it comparable with APRs in the U.S., it comes to 110%. That's because Azteca charges interest on the full amount borrowed throughout the life of the loan, even as the principal declines—not on the declining balance, as is common in the U.S. An adjunct professor at Columbia University's School of International and Public Affairs, Waterfield has no relationship with Azteca.

When Azteca loans go bad, the results can be bruising for borrowers. Porfirio Soriano Pérez and his son Zalatiel bought a $1,435 Chinese-made motorcycle last year, on an 18-month plan that required $29 weekly payments. They intended to use the bike to scout out customers for the parsley they grow on several acres just outside San Martín Texmelucan. The Sorianos knew the 68% financing would boost the motorcycle's total cost to $2,289, but they lacked cash to pay up front.

In February, disaster hit. A hailstorm wiped out their crop and with it their $350 monthly income. "Suddenly", says Porfirio, "we had nothing to sell, and no money." They fell behind on payments. Soon a collection agent began showing up at the extended Soriano family's unpainted home. In October, Azteca delivered written warning of legal action. "The problem is that people go into the store and buy out of pure emotion," says Morales, chief of Azteca's local legal department.

The Sorianos already had paid $1,560 on the motorcycle—more than the original sticker price—and owed about $700 more, but ended up returning the purchase. That erased the debt in Porfirio's name. The company will resell the bike and recover the money its owed. The Sorianos, meanwhile, have nothing left to plant a new crop.

Periodical Bibliography

The following articles have been selected to supplement the diverse views presented in this chapter.

Antoaneta Bezlova   "Micro Model for Mega-Country," *Asia Times*, October 26, 2006.

Krishna P.   "Commentary: Grameen Bank: Micro-Credit
Bhattacharjee   for Marginalized Families," *Berkeley Daily Planet*, December 22, 2006.

Tyler Cowen   "Microloans May Work, but There Is Dispute in India Over Who Will Make Them," *New York Times*, August 10, 2006.

Daniel Gross   "Poverty: Cheap Loans at Insanely High Rates? Give Us More," *Newsweek*, September 20, 2008.

Steve Hamm   "Capitalism with a Human Face," *BusinessWeek*, December 8, 2008.

Barbara Kiviat   "The Big Trouble in Small Loans," *TIME*, June 5, 2008.

Elizabeth Olson   "When Banks Say No, Microlenders Say Yes," *New York Times*, March 12, 2009.

Mark Sappenfield   "Big Banks Find Little Loans a Nobel Winner,
and Mark Trumbull   Too," *Christian Science Monitor*, October 16, 2006.

Laura Starita   "The Real Impacts of Micro-Credit," *Philanthropy Action*, October 18, 2008.

Sally Williams   "The Problems with Micro-Lending," *Berkeley Daily Planet*, January 26, 2007.

For Further Discussion

Chapter 1

1. This chapter illustrates how the landscape of alternative lending has expanded in response to the current credit crunch. Do you think the expansion of the loan market will have beneficial effects for American consumers once the credit crunch is over? If so, what might some of these benefits be?

2. Many commentators have blamed the mortgage crisis on lenders who offered subprime mortgages, and the lack of regulations governing these types of loans. After reading about the benefits of alternative loans, as well as some of the risks, do you think alternative lending should be subject to more government regulation? Explain your answer.

Chapter 2

1. One of the most prominent debates concerning payday lending is whether these lenders should be allowed to charge borrowers such high interest rates. After reading the viewpoints in this chapter, do you feel that consumers should be protected from payday lenders by laws limiting interest rates, as argued by Alexander Bartik et al., or allowed to make their own choices about payday loans, as argued by George Leef?

2. Payday lending is currently banned by fifteen states in America. Do you think bans on payday loans are more advantageous, or disadvantageous, to borrowers? Explain your answer.

Chapter 3

1. After reading viewpoints by Laura Vanderkam and Michelle Singletary, do you feel you might be inclined to lend money online if you were in a position to do so? Why or why not?

2. Can you think of any individual or social benefits of online peer lending that aren't mentioned in any of the viewpoints in this chapter? What are they?

3. After reading the viewpoints by Stacy Teicher Khadaroo and Eileen Ambrose, which do you find more convincing? Do you think online peer lending should be subject to government oversight or left alone? Explain your answer.

Chapter 4

1. After reading the first three viewpoints in this chapter, what capacity do you think microfinance has to end poverty? Is microcredit's potential overblown, or not? Explain your answer.

2. Since microcredit companies such as Grameen Bank often lend to more women than men, many have hailed microfinance as a force for gender equity. After reading the viewpoints by Zarina Geloo and Susan F. Feiner and Drucilla K. Barker, do you think this is true? Why?

3. Many critics argue that while microcredit companies offer better interest rates than local loan sharks, they still charge exorbitant rates that exploit borrowers' circumstances. Do you think microfinance companies ought to offer interest rates closer to bank rates, or are they justified in charging higher rates? Explain your answer.

Organizations to Contact

The editors have compiled the following list of organizations concerned with the issues debated in this book. The descriptions are derived from materials provided by the organizations. All have publications or information available for interested readers. The list was compiled on the date of publication of the present volume; the information provided here may change. Be aware that many organizations take several weeks or longer to respond to inquiries, so allow as much time as possible.

Americans for Fairness in Lending (AFFIL)

7 Winthrop Square, 4th Floor, Boston, MA 02110
(617) 841-8000
e-mail: info@affil.org
Web site: www.affil.org

Americans for Fairness in Lending (AFFIL) is a coalition of individuals and organizations dedicated to reforming the lending industry and the laws that regulate it to protect borrowers and their financial assets. AFFIL educates borrowers about their rights, alerts them to unfair lending practices, and lobbies for better legal safeguards on lenders. The organization's Web site publishes a blog, consumer news, action alerts, and press releases.

Board of Governors of the Federal Reserve System

Twentieth Street and Constitution Avenue NW
Washington, DC 20551
(202) 452-3000
Web site: www.federalreserve.gov

The Federal Reserve is the central bank of the United States. Its main functions are to maintain the stability of the U.S. financial system, guide the country's monetary policy, and supervise and regulate U.S. banks. The Federal Reserve publishes the *Federal Reserve Bulletin*, the *International Journal of Central Banking*, *Consumer's Guide to Mortgage Refinancings*, and *Consumer Handbook to Credit Protection Laws*.

Center for Responsible Lending (CRL)

302 West Main Street, Durham, NC   27701
(919) 313-8500
Web site: www.responsiblelending.org

The Center for Responsible Lending (CRL) is a nonprofit, nonpartisan research and policy organization concerned with protecting families from harmful lending practices. CRL provides knowledge and research to advocates, policy makers, and regulators, and works with partner organizations to litigate predatory lending and to reform the lending industry. CRL publishes reports, such as *Phantom Demand of Payday Loans* and *Predatory Profiling*, and fact sheets that detail the latest foreclosure numbers and the basics of payday lending.

Community Financial Services Association of America (CFSA)

515 King Street, Suite 300, Alexandria, VA   22314
(703) 684-1029 • fax: (703) 684-1219
Web site: www.cfsa.net

Community Financial Services Association of America (CFSA) is a trade organization representing the payday advance industry. CFSA works to protect consumers' access to payday lending services while advocating for responsible lending practices and regulation of these practices. CFSA publishes resources for consumers such as *Your Guide to Responsible Use of Payday Advances* and materials for policy makers and the media, such as *Payday Advance: Fact vs. Fiction*.

Credit Union National Association (CUNA)

5710 Mineral Point Road, Madison, WI   53705
(800) 356-9655
Web site: www.cuna.org

The Credit Union National Association (CUNA) is the foremost trade organization representing credit unions in the United States. CUNA provides information, advocacy, and professional development to credit unions and their employees. Its publications include *Credit Union Magazine*, *Credit Union Directors Newsletter*, and *Credit Union Front Line Newsletter*.

Mortgage Bankers Association (MBA)

1331 L Street NW, Washington, DC 20005

(202) 557-2700

Web site: www.mbaa.org

The Mortgage Bankers Association (MBA) represents the real estate finance industry in the United States. MBA provides information to its members, advocates for its lenders, and promotes fair lending practices. The association's publications include outlooks and forecasts, weekly economic commentaries, benchmarking studies, and industry overviews.

National Association of Student Financial Aid Administrators (NASFAA)

1101 Connecticut Avenue NW, Suite 1100

Washington, DC 20036

(202) 785-0453 • fax: (202) 785-1487

Web site: www.nasfaa.org

National Association of Student Financial Aid Administrators (NASFAA) is a nonprofit membership organization representing financial aid professionals at postsecondary educational institutions across the United States. Its primary goal is to help members deliver maximum funding and effective financial assistance to students in the United States. NASFAA's publications include the *Journal of Student Financial Aid*, the magazine *Student Aid Transcript*, and monographs for financial aid professionals.

National Credit Union Administration (NCUA)
1775 Duke Street, Alexandria, VA   22314
(703) 518-6300
Web site: www.ncua.gov

The National Credit Union Administration (NCUA) is an independent federal agency overseeing federal credit unions and insuring the savings of their account holders. NCUA provides information and resources to credit unions and their customers. Among the NCUA's publications are the *Consumer Compliance Self Assessment Guide, Facts About Federal Credit Unions,* and *How Your Accounts Are Federally Insured.*

U.S. Department of Housing and Urban Development (HUD)
451 Seventh Street SW, Washington, DC   20410
(202) 708-1112
Web site: www.hud.gov

The U.S. Department of Housing and Urban Development (HUD) is a government agency devoted to increasing home-ownership and ensuring access to affordable housing for all citizens. HUD works with community- and faith-based organizations to help realize these goals. Among HUD's publications are *Subprime Lending and Alternative Financial Service Providers: A Literature Review and Empirical Analysis, The American Housing Survey and Non-Traditional Mortgage Products,* and *Assessing Problems of Default in Local Mortgage Markets.*

U.S. Securities and Exchange Commission (SEC)
100 F Street NE, Washington, DC   20549
(202) 942-8088
Web site: www.sec.gov

The U.S. Securities and Exchange Commission (SEC) is a government agency designed to protect investors and maintain fair and orderly financial markets. It does this primarily by educating consumers about investment opportunities and the laws governing them, and enforcing these laws. The SEC's publications include the daily *SEC News Digest* and studies such as the congressionally mandated *Study on Mark-to-Market Accounting.*

Woodstock Institute

29 East Madison, Suite 1710, Chicago, IL   60602
(312) 368-0310 • fax: (312) 368-0316
Web site: www.woodstockinst.org

Woodstock Institute is a policy and advocacy organization promoting community investment and economic development in low-income and minority communities, with specific focus on increasing affordable housing and small business development in these areas. The institute provides research, education, and analysis, and it partners with other organizations to meet these goals. It publishes fact sheets, foreclosure updates, and research reports such as *Paying More for the American Dream III: Promoting Responsible Lending to Lower-Income Communities and Communities of Color* and *The Illinois Payday Loan Loophole.*

Bibliography of Books

Beatriz Armendáriz and Jonathan Morduch

The Economics of Microfinance. Cambridge, MA: MIT Press, 2010.

Richard Bitner

Confessions of a Subprime Lender: An Insider's Tale of Greed, Fraud, and Ignorance. Hoboken, NJ: Wiley, 2008.

Patrick Bolton and Howard Rosenthal, eds.

Credit Markets for the Poor. New York: Russell Sage, 2005.

James H. Carr and Zhong Yi Tong, eds.

Replicating Microfinance in the United States. Washington, DC: Woodrow Wilson Center Press, 2002.

Alan Michael Collinge

The Student Loan Scam: The Most Oppressive Debt in U.S. History—and How We Can Fight Back. Boston, MA: Beacon Press, 2009.

Jane L. Collins, Micaela di Leonardo, and Brett Williams, eds.

New Landscapes of Inequality: Neoliberalism and the Erosion of Democracy in America. Santa Fe, NM: School for Advanced Research Press, 2008.

Alex Counts

Small Loans, Big Dreams: How Nobel Prize Winner Muhammad Yunus and Microfinance Are Changing the World. Hoboken, NJ: Wiley, 2008.

Edward M. Gramlich

Subprime Mortgages: America's Latest Boom and Bust. Washington, DC: Urban Institute Press, 2007.

David Hulme and Thankom Arun, eds. *Microfinance: A Reader.* New York: Routledge, 2009.

Dan Immergluck *Credit to the Community: Community Reinvestment and Fair Lending Policy in the United States.* Armonk, NY: M.E. Sharpe, 2004.

Dan Immergluck *Foreclosed: High-Risk Lending, Deregulation, and the Undermining of America's Mortgage Market.* Ithaca, NY: Cornell University Press, 2009.

Howard Karger *Shortchanged: Life and Debt in the Fringe Economy.* San Francisco, CA: Berrett-Koehler Publishers, 2005.

Paul Krugman *The Return of Depression Economics and the Crisis of 2008.* New York: W.W. Norton, 2009.

Richard Lord *American Nightmare: Predatory Lending and the Foreclosure of the American Dream.* Monroe, ME: Common Courage Press, 2005.

Robert D. Manning *Credit Card Nation: The Consequences of America's Addiction to Credit.* New York: Basic Books, 2000.

Adam Michaelson *The Foreclosure of America: The Inside Story of the Rise and Fall of Countrywide Home Loans, the Mortgage Crisis, and the Default of the American Dream.* New York: Berkley, 2009.

Paul Muolo and Mathew Padilla	*Chain of Blame: How Wall Street Caused the Mortgage and Credit Crisis.* Hoboken, NJ: Wiley, 2008.
Kevin Phillips	*Bad Money: Reckless Finance, Failed Politics, and the Global Crisis of American Capitalism.* New York: Viking, 2008.
Nicolas P. Retsinas and Eric S. Belsky, eds.	*Borrowing to Live: Consumer and Mortgage Credit Revisited.* Washington, DC: Brookings Institution Press, 2008.
Nicolas P. Retsinas and Eric S. Belsky, eds.	*Building Assets, Building Credit: Creating Wealth in Low-Income Communities.* Washington, DC: Brookings Institution Press, 2005.
Marguerite S. Robinson	*The Microfinance Revolution: Sustainable Finance for the Poor.* Washington, DC: World Bank Publications, 2001.
Marguerite S. Robinson	*The Microfinance Revolution, Volume 2: Lessons from Indonesia.* Washington, DC: World Bank Publications, 2002.
Stephen L. Ross and John Yinger	*The Color of Credit: Mortgage Discrimination, Research Methodology, and Fair-Lending Enforcement.* Cambridge, MA: MIT Press, 2003.
Stuart Rutherford	*The Pledge: ASA, Peasant Politics, and Microfinance in the Development of Bangladesh.* New York: Oxford University Press USA, 2009.

James D. Scurlock *Maxed Out: Hard Times in the Age of Easy Credit.* New York: Scribner, 2007.

Phil Smith and Eric Thurman *A Billion Bootstraps: Microcredit, Barefoot Banking, and the Business Solution for Ending Poverty.* New York: McGraw-Hill, 2007.

Gregory D. Squires, ed. *Why the Poor Pay More: How to Stop Predatory Lending.* Westport, CT: Praeger, 2004.

Guy Stuart *Discriminating Risk: The U.S. Mortgage Lending Industry in the Twentieth Century.* Ithaca, NY: Cornell University Press, 2003.

Stuart Vyse *Going Broke: Why Americans Can't Hold on to Their Money.* New York: Oxford University Press USA, 2008.

Brett Williams *Debt for Sale: A Social History of the Credit Trap.* Philadelphia, PA: University of Pennsylvania Press, 2004.

Muhammad Yunus *Banker to the Poor: Micro-Lending and the Battle Against World Poverty.* New York: PublicAffairs, 2007.

Index

A

AARP (American Association of Retired People), 33, 35
Abate, Tom, 47
Abbot, Steve, 61, 66
Adjustable-rate mortgages, 38
Advance America Cash Advance Centers, Inc. (payday lender), 72
AfricaNews, 151
Agarwal, Akash, 111
Air Force *Times* newspaper, 67
Alligheri, Dante, 50
"Alternative Lenders Profit as Banks Close Their Doors" (Lynch), 14
Alternative loans/lending
    advantages of, 20–25
    attractiveness of, 28–30
    risks of, 26–31, 38–39
    as threat to banks, 24–25
    types of, 22–24
Alternative mortgages
    Boreczky on, 37
    delinquency rates, 37
    piggyback loans, 34
    traditional vs., 32–39
Altman, Edward, 28
Ambrose, Eileen, 114–118
American Bankers Association, 25
American dream, 41
American Home Mortgage company, 14
"America's Growing Fringe Economy" (Karger), 42
Ameriquest mortgage company, 14
Amsden, Alice, 138–139

"An End to Payday Loans?" (Sheppard), 81
Annual percentage rates (APRs), 79–81
Anti-Predatory Lending Protection Act, 66
Army *Times* newspaper, 67
Ayers, David, 15–16

B

Banamex (Mexican bank), 170
Banco Azteca (Latin America), 169–179
BanComún la Frontera micro-lender (Mexico), 162–163
Banking, Housing, and Urban Affairs Committee, 37
Bank of America (BAC), 95
Bankrate.com, 24, 111
Bankruptcies
    investment firms, 30
    Mexican lenders, 177
    during mortgage crisis, 54–56
    payday loans, 55
Bankruptcies during mortgage crisis, 14
Banks
    bulge bracket investment banks, 27
    charities vs., 101–102
    closing of, 14
    credit crunch of, 29
    developmental banks, 138–139
    microcredit lenders vs., 123, 140–141